Doreen Frances Richmond
Big Ideas For A Small Bedroom

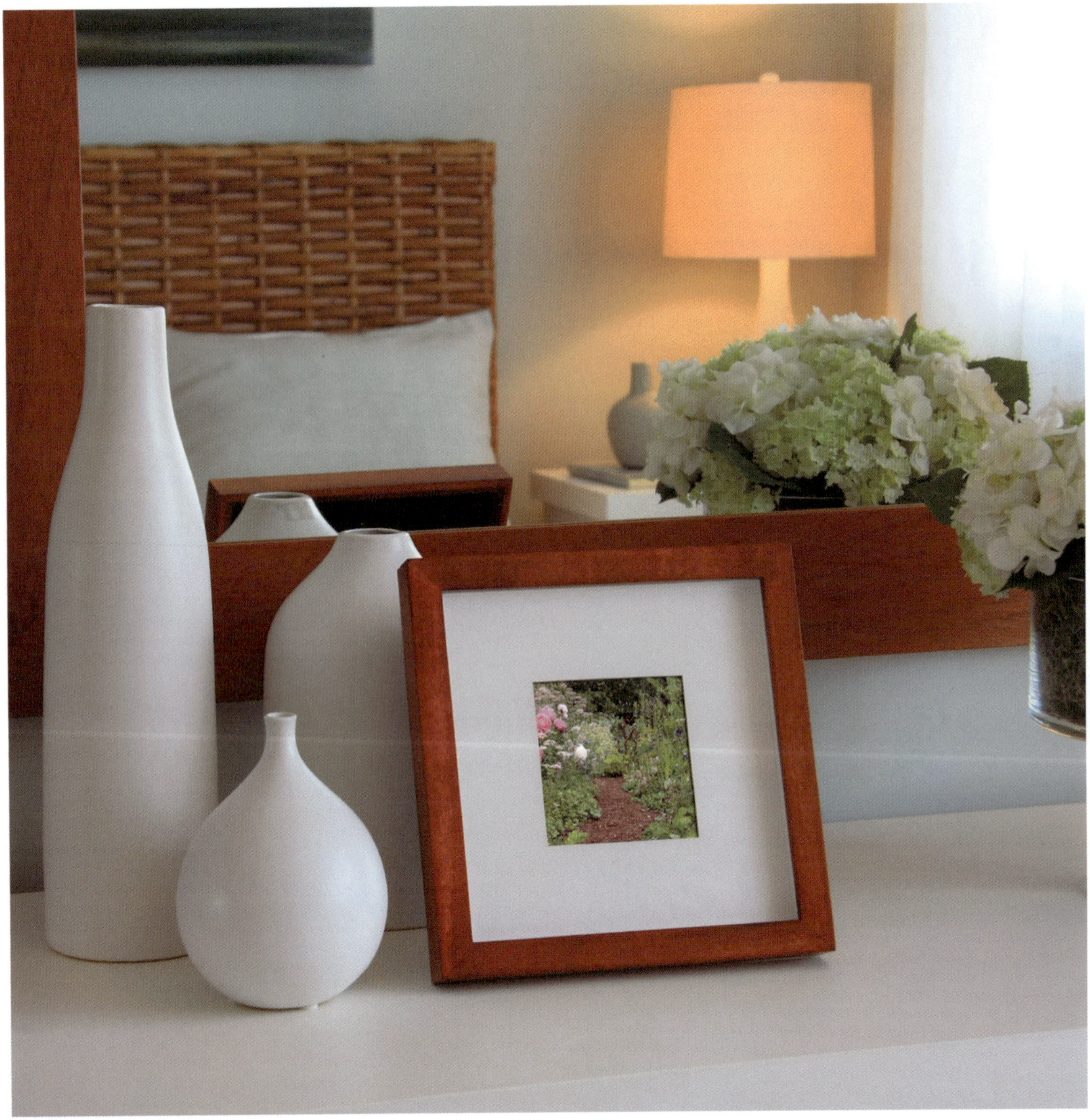

Thank you

I always read or hear that if you start out to create something that is well out of your comfort zone, the support you need will be there. Although I have encountered this numerous times, I was nevertheless deeply touched when I experienced so much help as I set out to write this book. My gratitude goes to the following people who made it possible.

The idea was initiated when working with my mentor, Denise Wakeman. Her enthusiasm fired me into action. The other members of the group who were training with Denise: Angie, Kim-G, Kim-W, Michelle, Penny, Rebecca and Sara were so supportive, not only through their own exceptional activities, but also with their encouragement and cheering-on.

Since this was a book requiring lots of graphic work, I knew that I could not realize this project without the support of Frauke. Despite her tight time-table, she set time apart to put the concept into a delightfully attractive form and injected many ideas. It was the speed with which she worked and the creative interest she expressed that encouraged me to stay focused and to accomplish the project.

My thanks also go to the talented interior designers who generously contributed to this book with examples of their work; and to the many photographers whose engaging photos made it possible to create this poetic and expressive book.

Thank you all very much.

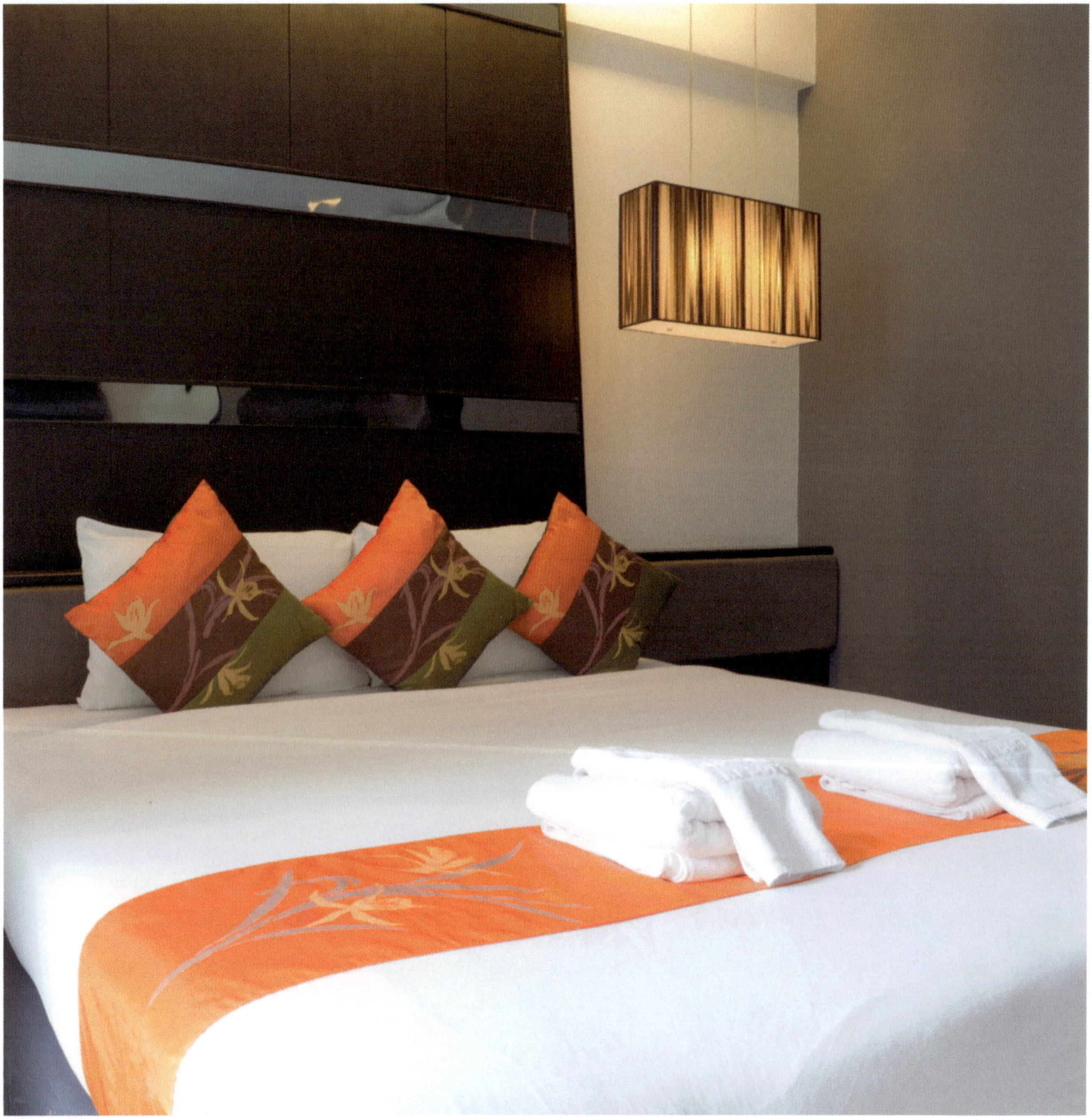

Big Ideas For The Small Bedroom

Table Of Contents

11	|	Introduction: Why The Small Bedroom?
15	|	Choosing A Color Scheme For The Small Bedroom
19	|	Color Harmony And Rhythm Add Impact To Any Room
23	|	Which Color For The Walls?
27	|	Different Tastes In Color Can Create Conflict

The Fragility Of White

33	|	White For Timeless Elegance And Simplicity
41	|	Black And White Create An Elegant Impact
47	|	Black And White Eternity
51	|	Gray And Off-White Give An Exclusive Touch

Blues For The Small Bedroom

59 | Danish Design And Blue Add Spaciousness To The Small Bedroom
64 | Maritime Blue Enchants The Small Bedroom
70 | Monochromatic Harmonies

Bold Energy Colors

74 | Dark Red Adds A Striking Elegance To The Small Room
82 | Big And Bold With Orange
84 | Neighboring Colors Like Each Other
87 | Orange Portrays All The Gorgeous Warm Tones Of Autumn
92 | The Dramatic Energy Of A Museum

Complementary Color Schemes Add A Colorful Impact

98 | Red And Green
102 | Blue And Orange
106 | Purple And Yellow
111 | Swerving Tulips Add A Colorful Zest
112 | With Pink and Green It Is Spring Time All Year Round

Moods Created By Color

122 | Rococo Pastels Add A Romantic Touch To The Small Bedroom
129 | Violet Creates A Contemplative Mood
136 | Green For A Peaceful Refuge
142 | Turquoise Serenity

148 | Rich Chocolate Brown For A Calming Ambiance
159 | Naturals Add A Subtle Distinction To Small Spaces

Important Details

166 | Colors And Styles For The Windows
174 | Venetian Blinds, Plisse Shades
182 | Bed Linen

Credits

186 | Interior Designer Credits
190 | Photography Credits

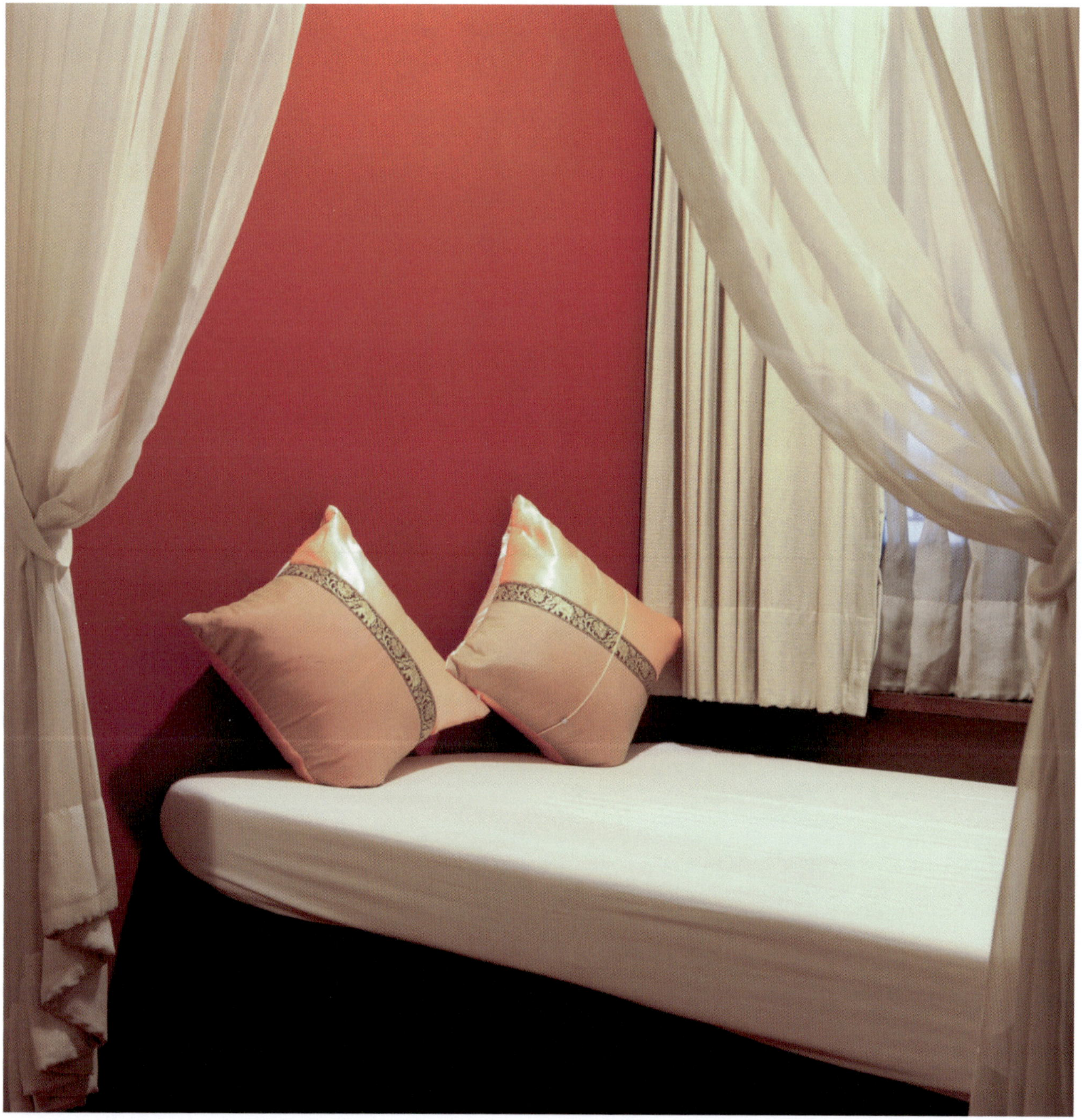

Introduction: Why The Small Bedroom?

Although the bedroom is not always the main focus in a home, it should be. And the spare room for the guest equally as such. This is perhaps the only place in the home where we can fall into deep relaxation and let go of all the busy activities that surround us. It is here that we can experience our true nature, where we are the most vulnerable. A beautiful surrounding creates a peace that reaches deep down within us and gives us a sense of being at one with ourselves and the world. This is where we prepare for the next day, refreshing both mind and body. It is where couples open up to each other in sexual union and share some of most precious moments of their lives.

It is an extremely intimate space, sometimes even a sanctuary where we gain not only physical and mental strength, but also a spiritual refreshing. This room should be designed as such.

We spend at least one third of our day in this area. This is where we find recuperation and regain our emotional stability and a sense of wellness. The smaller the room, the more effort is required to make it a beautiful, intimate space. It has to function well, which means avoidance of clutter. And it needs a well thought out color scheme – even a special theme – so the small bedroom can expand far beyond its four walls, at least from the perspective of conscious design.

Everyone has a particular style that matches their personality and that is why this book not only shows meditative concepts, but also charming, perky ideas.

The small rooms rarely get the attention their larger counterparts receive. It often seems that all the energy goes into the large scheme and there is none left to create the small spaces and transform them into something very special. Especially in the cities, the living spaces are becoming rare and often much smaller; and sometimes the main bedroom is extremely small as well.

With this book, I hope to inspire you to make this small bedroom into a very special place indeed. A place in your home that can proudly stand next to those super luxurious bedrooms you see in magazines; and a place of comfort and refuge.

Color is such a vast subject but I have included the most important aspects in this book, which will help the beginner to create their own color scheme for a room. Applied well, colors can add a very special quality and touch of luxury to any space at a very low cost.

This book concentrates on creating style for a small bedroom. Space plays a vital role in a confined space. Generally, it it important to avoid clutter by having sufficient storage and eliminating any pieces of furniture that are not sufficiently functional. There is normally only sufficient space for basics, such as the bed, wardrobe and a bedside table. A wardrobe that protrudes from the wall can look very heavy in a small space and overpower a room. Ideally a wall to wall wardrobe with sliding doors from ceiling to floor will look more spacious and provide plenty of storage. Panels made of a strong material, fixed to a ceiling trailer, are a good alternative. Even though these basics are used in most of the interior designs in this book, you will be surprised to see how versatile the possibilities are for creating an individual and stylish bedroom.

|13

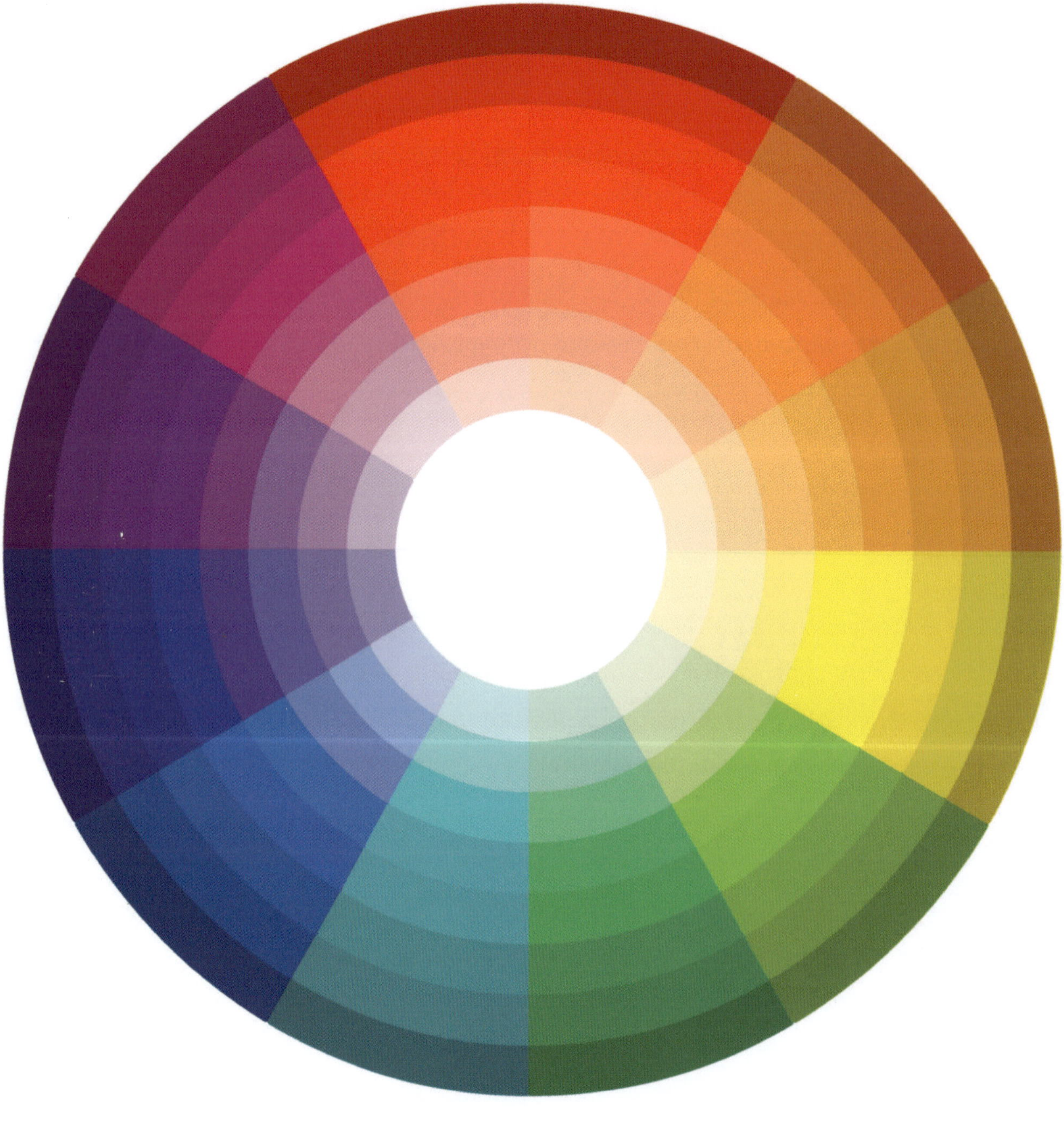

Choosing A Color For The Small Bedroom

When you go to a paint store to choose a color, you will often be presented with a color matching system to help you with your choice. Most people feel totally overwhelmed by the abundance of possibilities, and feel fairly frustrated when they try to choose a suitable color.

Understanding how a color matching system is compiled will help you to use it more effectively. There are actually only six colors which result in the approximately 1000 hues you find within a color system. These are yellow, orange, red, violet, blue and green. These colors are mixed with black and/or white which result in the tremendous diversity of hues.

Each major color has three distinct shades, from cool to warm. Blue, for example, has a warm violet blue shade, a pure sky blue and a cooler shade which is turquoise. There are also three major shades of primal red, these being a fiery orange red, a pure red, and a cooler red with a bluish tint.

With yellow, there is a cool lemon yellow, a pure yellow and a warm sunflower yellow.

The three shades of green are a warm spring green, pure green and a cooler blue-green. Each of these hues develops many shades when mixed with black and/or white. However, the intensity of warmth or coolness will remain when they are mixed with black or white. For example, a warm spring green will turn into a warm olive green; a cool red will turn into a cool wine red, a warm orange red will turn into a warm rusty red. This is important to consider when you are combining chromatic colors. A warm rusty red will look great with a warm orange red because it belongs to the same color family. The same warm rusty red will clash with a cool wine red.

Before you actually try to choose a hue from a color matching system, it is useful first to decide upon the color that suits your need. When you have decided upon the color, you can then use the color matching system to decide upon the exact shade of that particular color. This way, you will avoid the overwhelming sensation you experience when being confronted with the hundreds of hues contained in a color matching system.

DDLETON	245	FOWLER PINK	39	INCARNADINE 248	LANCASTER YELLOW 249	FARROW'S CREAM*	67	HAY
LAMINE	230	OINTMENT PINK	21	RECTORY RED 217	DAYROOM YELLOW 233	DORSET CREAM	68	CIARA YELLOW
NDER ROSE	246	RED EARTH	64	RADICCHIO 96	CITRON 74	PRINT ROOM YELLOW*	69	SUDBURY YELLOW
NK GROUND	202	PORPHYRY PINK	49	EATING ROOM RED 43	YELLOW GROUND 218	PALE HOUND	71	STRAW
ETTING PLASTER	231	TERRE D'EGYPTE	247	BOOK ROOM RED 50	BABOUCHE	LEMON	2	INDIA YELLOW

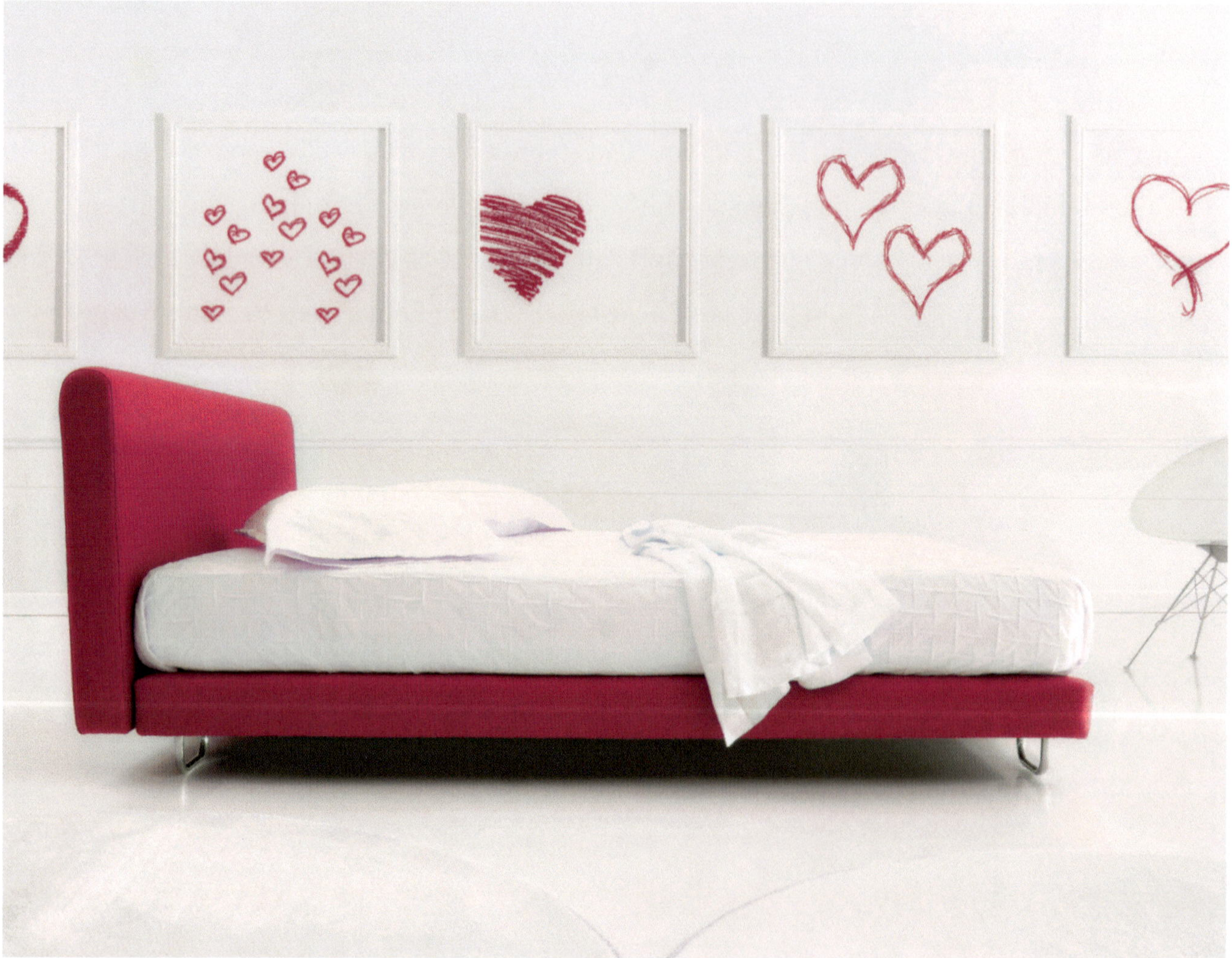

Color Harmony And Rhythm Add Impact To Any Room

Color and rhythm are extremely important for creating a peaceful living space. Many people are afraid of color, so keep everything neutral. Very few people are aware of rhythm, so things simply do not relate. A room can be very simple in its decoration, with very cheap furnishing, but if there is a good balance between color and rhythm, it will feel very pleasant and express harmony. A room furnished with the most expensive furniture and accessories will feel uncomfortable if color and rhythm are missing.

Color and rhythm are a biological requirement. When we enter a space, the eyes will immediately check out for everything that relates. It is instantly trying to have an organized view of the total area. This is part of the biological need for protection, coming from times when we spent most of the day out hunting.

The brain needs to be continually activated through colors. Colors are so important to the organism that they have a direct path to the hormone system to create immediate emotional response. This is why we react to color faster than we can think. A sudden awareness of an unusual color in nature could imply danger, we need to react quickly. When the brain is deprived of color, it will suffer from boredom. Over activation through disorganization of color and rhythm can cause nervousness and headaches.

These innate biological requirements are just as important to us in our interiors. They are also very inexpensive and easy to create. If there are three similar lamps placed at different parts of a room, this will create an organized feel, a sense of balance. If you have something in a bright red in one corner of the room, having a repetition of this in one or two other areas of the room will create a sense of unity. The eye can move easily throughout the space, conceive the total area quickly and gain a satisfying sense of harmony. Using color consciously will have an immediate impact on a room and instantly add the exact feel you wish to express for a sense of well-being.

Just using color and rhythm in a room, is all you require to make it aesthetically pleasing. Not even the most exquisite furniture can compete with these extremely inexpensive attributes. On the contrary, everything in the room will be made to appear of superb taste.

21

Which Color For The Walls?

Why do we often have problems deciding on a color for a room? For me, it is always interesting to make the same observation in my seminars, "Color for Living Spaces." So often, participants will reject a color, but when they start to create a collage with the very same color, their negative associations with it change to a positive experience.

Every color has a positive and negative side to it. If people reject a color, this is usually because they experience more of its negative aspects. For example, purple is often experienced as obscure and dim. During working on a collage with this hue, participants who reject the color will discover for the first time the tranquility, peace, depth and perception of purple.

When we reject a color, it is often because of its negative conceptions. This prevents us from experiencing the color from its positive side and consequently from using it in our surroundings.

Sometimes a person may have had a bad experience during the past that was somehow connected to that color. Every time they consciously see it the feeling, but not necessarily the experience itself, will come back into the present. In such cases, it is better to avoid the color, until the issue has been dealt with.

Our like or dislike of a color tells us a lot about ourselves. Every color stimulates us differently. If it harmonizes with our emotional state, we experience it as agreeable. However, if it creates discord with our feelings we will find it unpleasant. For example, some people are very energetic, extroverted and love vigorous sports, their tendency will often be to warm colors, such as red and orange. Blue may be rejected, because it is perceived as boring. Sometimes the color, and its qualities of peace, concentration and single-mindedness, can be exactly what they need to create balance in their lives. On the other hand, the warmer colors could match up perfectly with their temperament. It needs time and reflection to discover the right colors for a particular person.

We all experience the psychological aspects of colors. Some of us take time to become more aware of them. If you understand your relationship to the various colors, and can analyze what quality is required as a balance for your life situation, it will be easier to make color decisions. For couples who share the same bedroom, it is important to understand that each may feel more relaxed with a certain color. If there is discrepancy in choices and this is emotionally charged, then it would me most important to find a color both like, even if this means reverting to neutrals or white.

Everyone has a color they particular like.

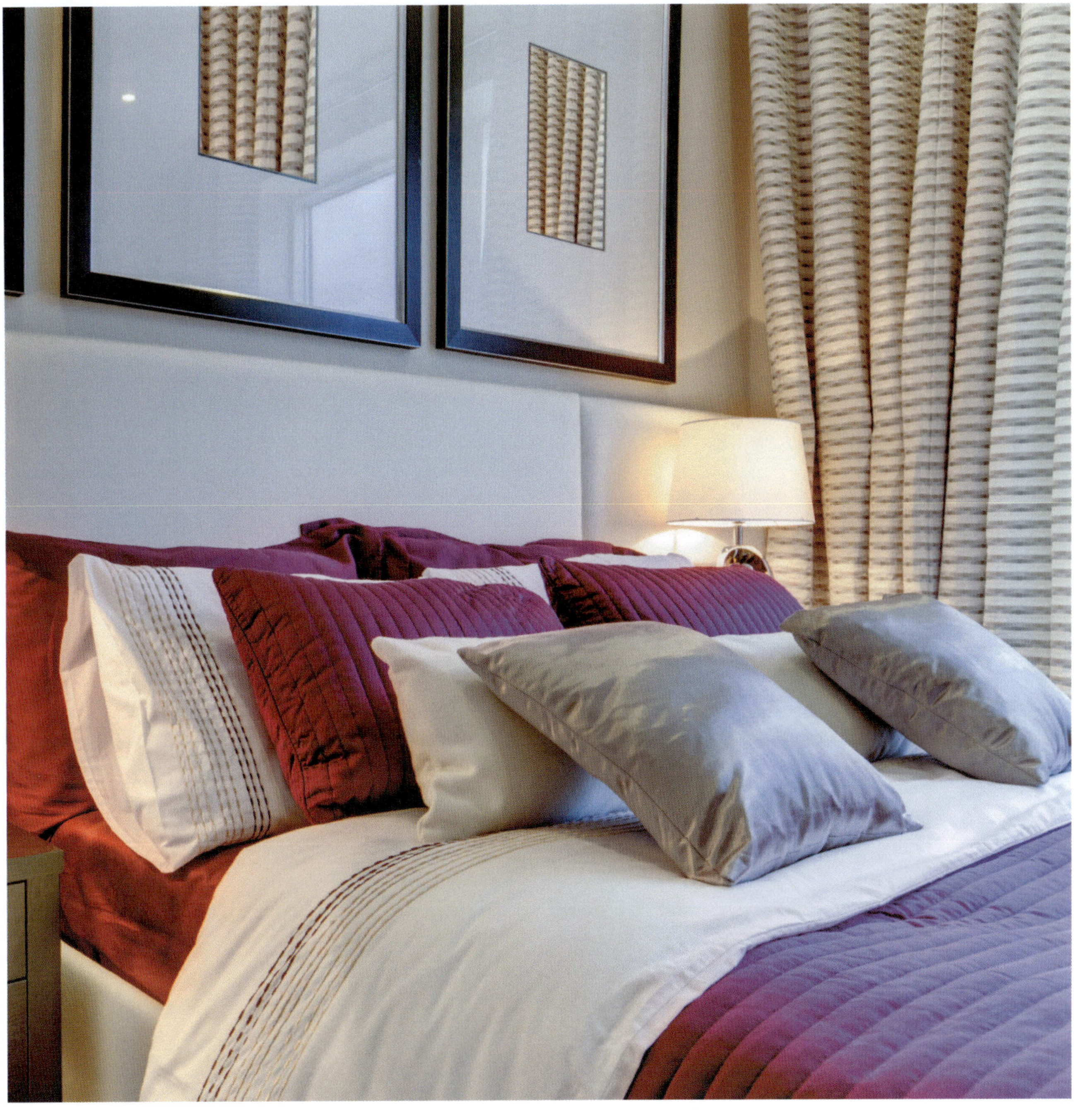

Different Needs – Different Styles

Some people love a touch of extravagance. This can easily be achieved with luxurious bed linen, especially when the room is small.

Different Tastes In Color Can Create Conflict

When couples come together to furnish a home, it can sometimes cause trouble, especially when color decisions are made. The one person loves a particular color, the other rejects it totally. This can result in some heavy discussion, even quarrels, about whether a color is in good taste or not.

Color preference is not only a question of taste but also a psychological mirror of how we feel. This is why the love of a color, or the disapproval, goes far deeper than aesthetics. As already mentioned, rejecting a color also means rejecting the positive energy connected with that particular color. For example, if you love orange you will be drawn to its positive qualities, such as outgoing, friendly, communicative, joyful and playful. If on the other hand, there is a strong rejection of the color, it will be seen as gaudy, loud and aggressive. This rejection could be a sign that the opposite qualities are required: those of peace, gentleness and relaxation.

Psychologically, every color has its negative or positive side, just like people. There is always some subjective association when colors are chosen, and it is seldom an objective decision. In addition to the colors themselves, the saturation of color plays an important role in decision making. A peaceful, calm, more introverted person will be attracted to softer hues; colors that are very light and possibly grayed down to give them a muted, neutral quality. This could be pale muted lilacs, blues or greens, off-whites and grays. Extroverted, energetic people will be attracted to gay, bright colors and want to surround themselves with a snazzy interior.

In order to avoid conflicts about choice, it is important to recognize the differences in taste and respect them. For example: A good way to understand the differences is for both partners to cut out pictures from magazines and make a collage. They must feel emotionally connected to the chosen pictures. These need not be themes of interior design.

Peaceful, introverted people will find themselves attracted to different colored images than to those of an extroverted partner. The collage exercise will reveal the amount of color a person feels comfortable with: the total feeling will be bright or muted. It would then be a good idea to study various interior design ideas and make a collage of the designs of rooms and elements one feels attracted to. Each partner should work separately.

If there is considerable difference in the choices, it will be necessary to work together on compromises. For a bedroom that is to be designed for both the introvert and extrovert, a good way of compromising, especially for a small room, would be to keep the main colors muted and then add one extravagant accent in the form of a large picture.

Every type of person and room require different needs and different tastes.

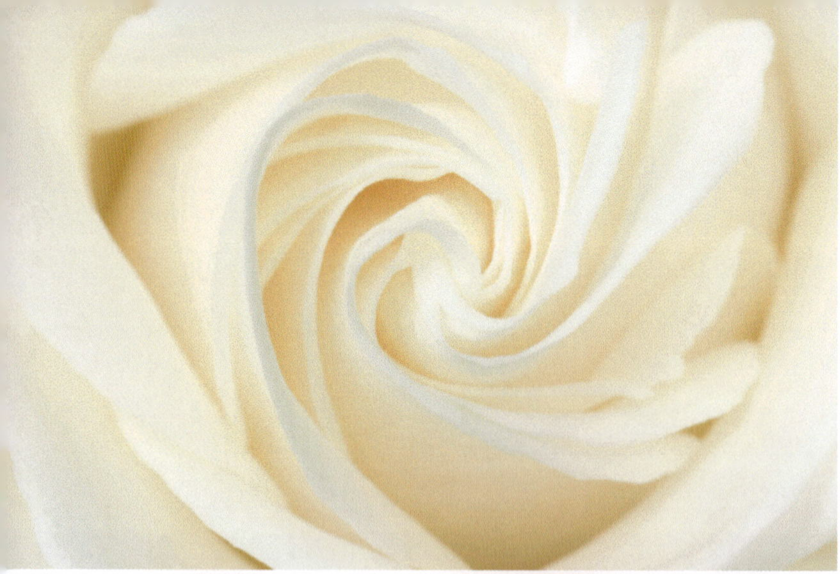

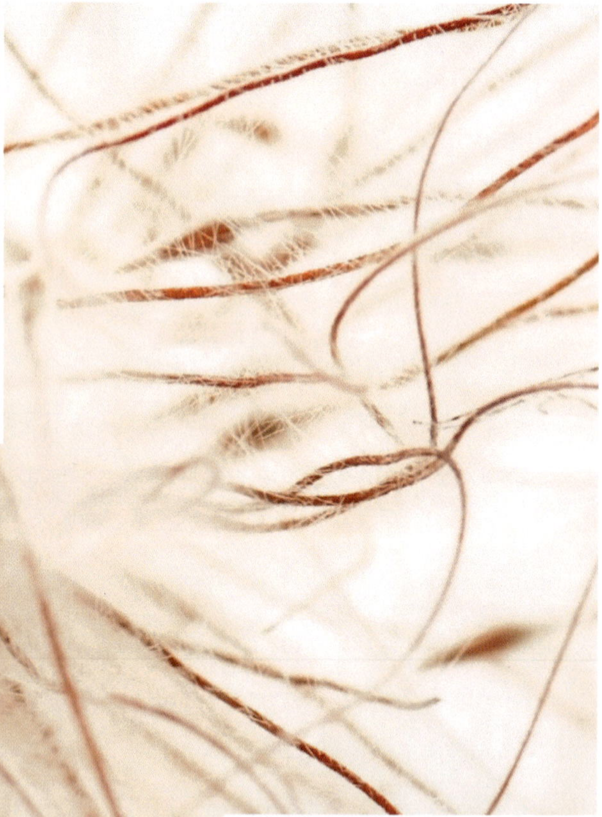

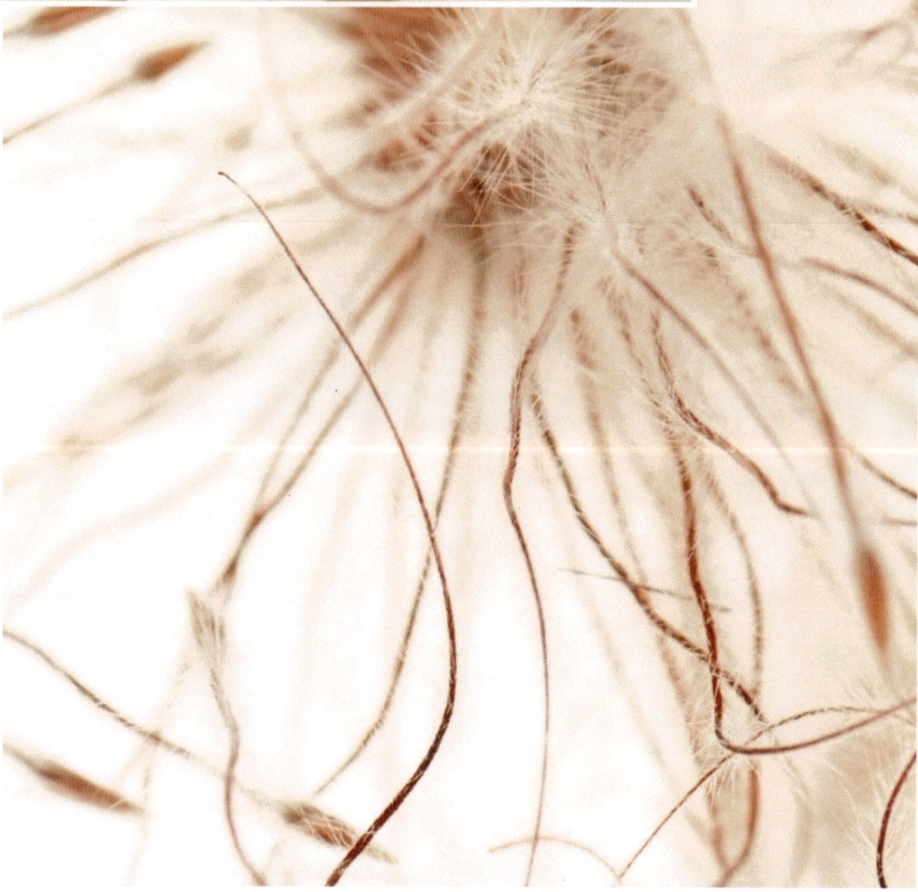

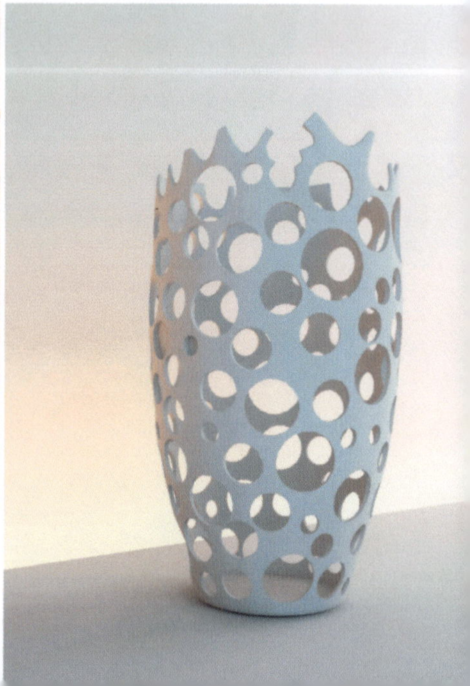

The Fragility Of White

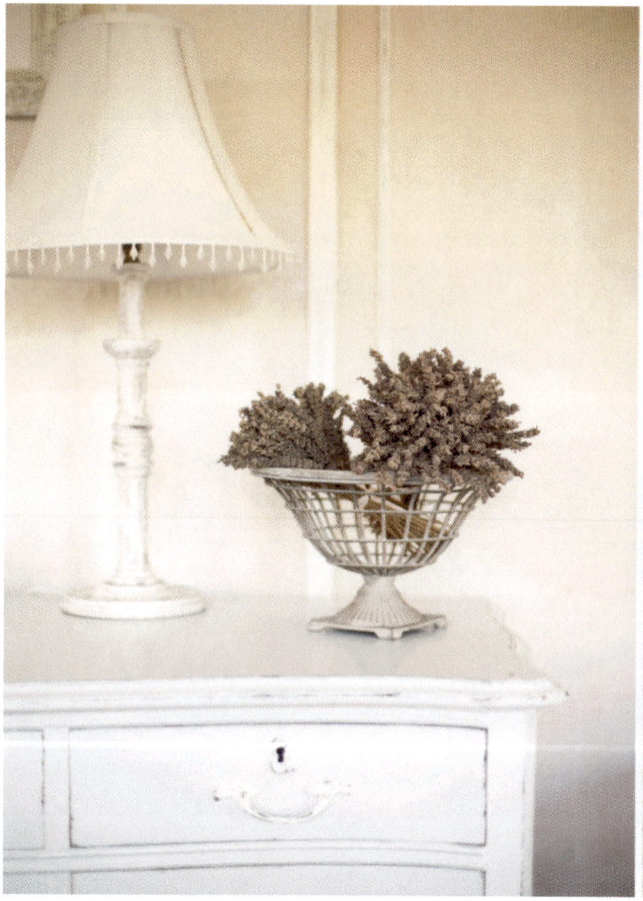
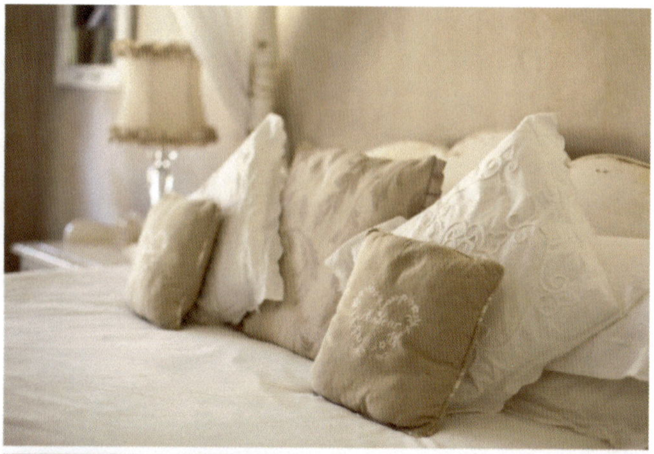
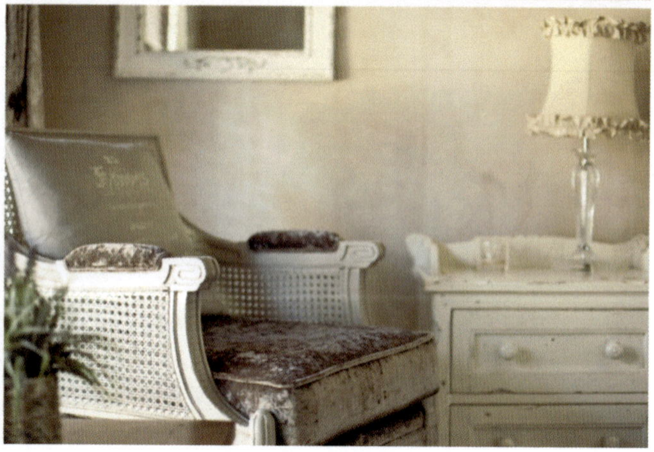

White For Timeless Elegance And Simplicity

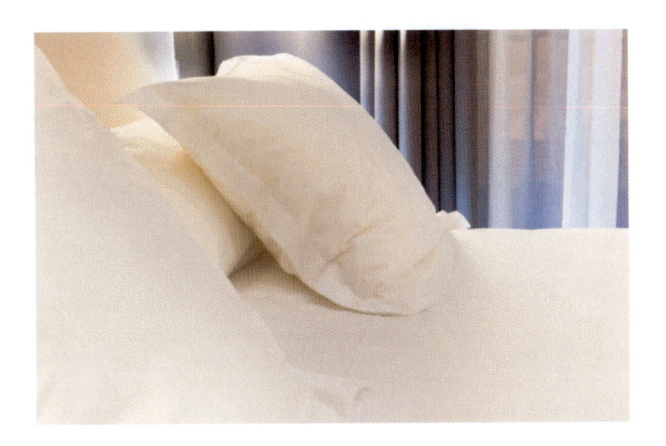

Because a room is small, we often tend to think that white is the answer: the absence of any emotional energy whatsoever. However, all white interiors are certainly not the answer for creating a calm surrounding. You will never find an environment that is totally white in nature. Such a landscape would actually be disturbing. Our eyes require the continual interaction of color, light, form and shadow.

On the other hand, over stimulation through too many colors, patterns or mix and match, can cause changes in the breathing, pulse rate, and make us very nervous; equally, under stimulation, such as monotonous, white, neutral surroundings can also cause irritation. The energy is pulled inwards and this can result in a negative emotional response, from boredom to anxiety. White surroundings are anything but neutral as far as the psychological experience is concerned.

Yet nevertheless, all white interiors, especially for the bedroom, are popular. They can be created so as to give a small space a timeless elegance and serenity. If you decide to go for this purist look, here are a few tips to ensure that there is a sense of peace and unity in the room and that you are not left feeling the room is just empty.

Texture plays an important role in such an environment. Consciously contrasting materials such as linen with silk, wood with glass, or soft wool with metal, will create a haptic quality. Using rhythm throughout the small room will equally add an interesting note. For example: Three white roses set individually into vases, pairs of lamps. And of course, the bed linen itself can be highly diversified, just by using different types of pillowcases, elaborately embroidered or with the pure simplicity of corded edges.

You can also counteract the aloof coldness of white by combining it with light beige or very pale gray. This combination will keep the room neutral and light, yet will add a new dimension to white. White against soft colors looks refreshingly beautiful and its symbolic meaning of purity and calmness will be accentuated. It will gain a look of crisp freshness.

Morning Tea ...

... And Time To Get Up

Add a little gray if the white feels too cool.

A space within a space: pure white and transparency have been chosen for this small bedroom area, thus allowing the vast space of the ocean to be the main focus of attention. It is not possible for many to have such a view, but a beautiful mural on the wall would at least allow you to recreate this meditative style

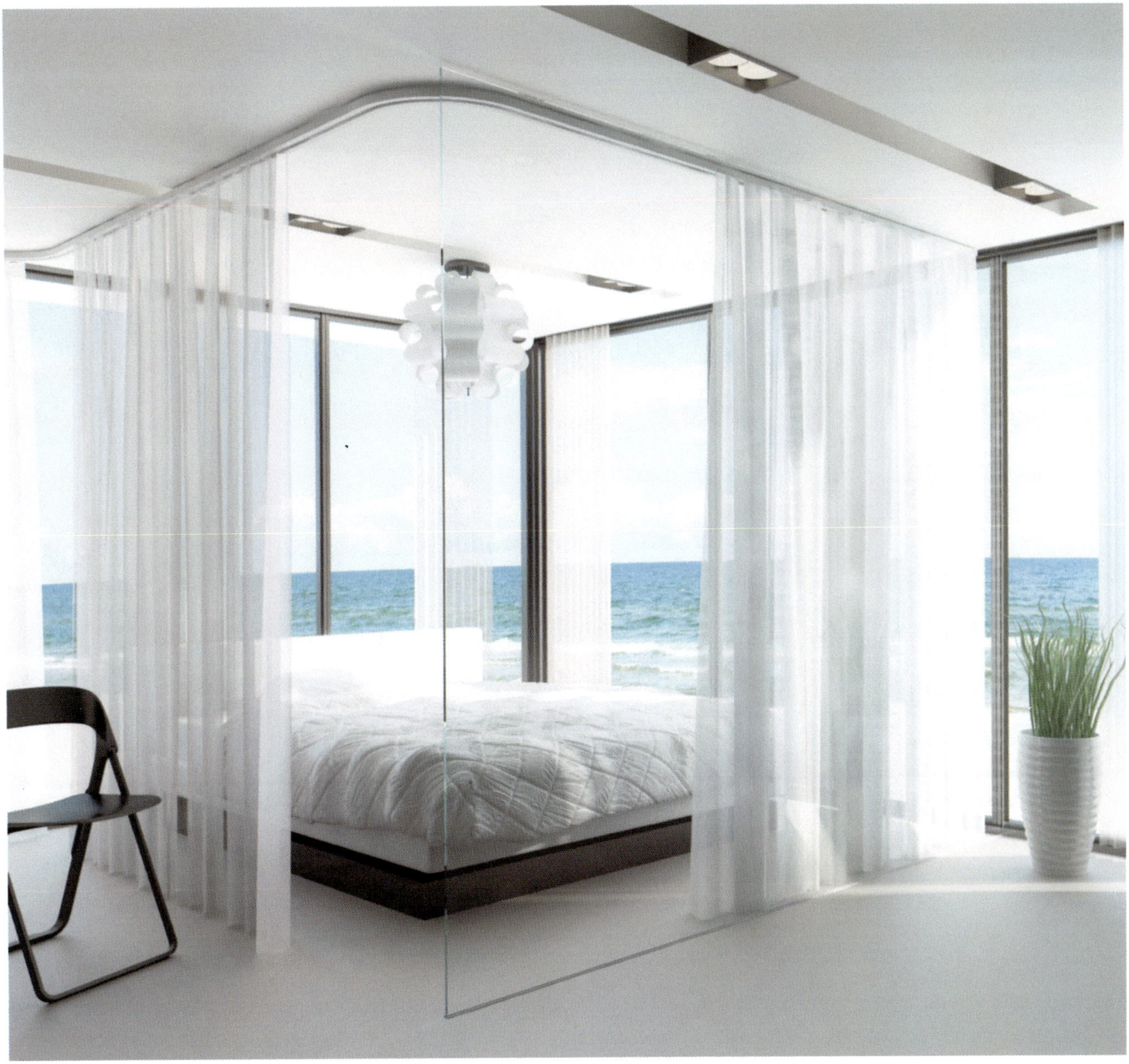

40

Black And White Create An Elegant Impact

Black and white are distinctive neutrals that allow for endless variations. By keeping the neutral scheme within this combination, it is very easy to decorate a small bedroom and make it an attractive and elegant haven. Small bedrooms must not be boring because there is a lack of space. On the contrary, by using dark and light contrasts effectively they can be transformed into interesting and impacting spaces.

Black and white are outstanding for creating an elegant simplicity or a theatrical impact. They allow for endless variations and styles. They can be applied to create a clear cut styling, a traditional country look, modern design or an individual agglomeration of various different objects and styles. When kept in black and white, the result will always be refined and attractive.

Accents of black and white for lamps, bed linen and pictures will create an exciting rhythm of light and dark. Depending on your taste, you can also add a theme to your black and white environment. Almost every subject is available as a black and white print or photograph. If you love music, you can collect photos of musicians; animal lovers will find some fascinating photographs of wild animals or of the much loved domestic cat or dog. There are so many different animals with black and white markings that a collection of such animal photographs can add humor and fun to the room's decor. Trees or landscapes, boats or seascapes, are also ideal themes for the decoration.

Black and white are very versatile and even though they are often preferred for minimalistic room designs, they look as equally good when applied to a romantic theme.

|43

44|

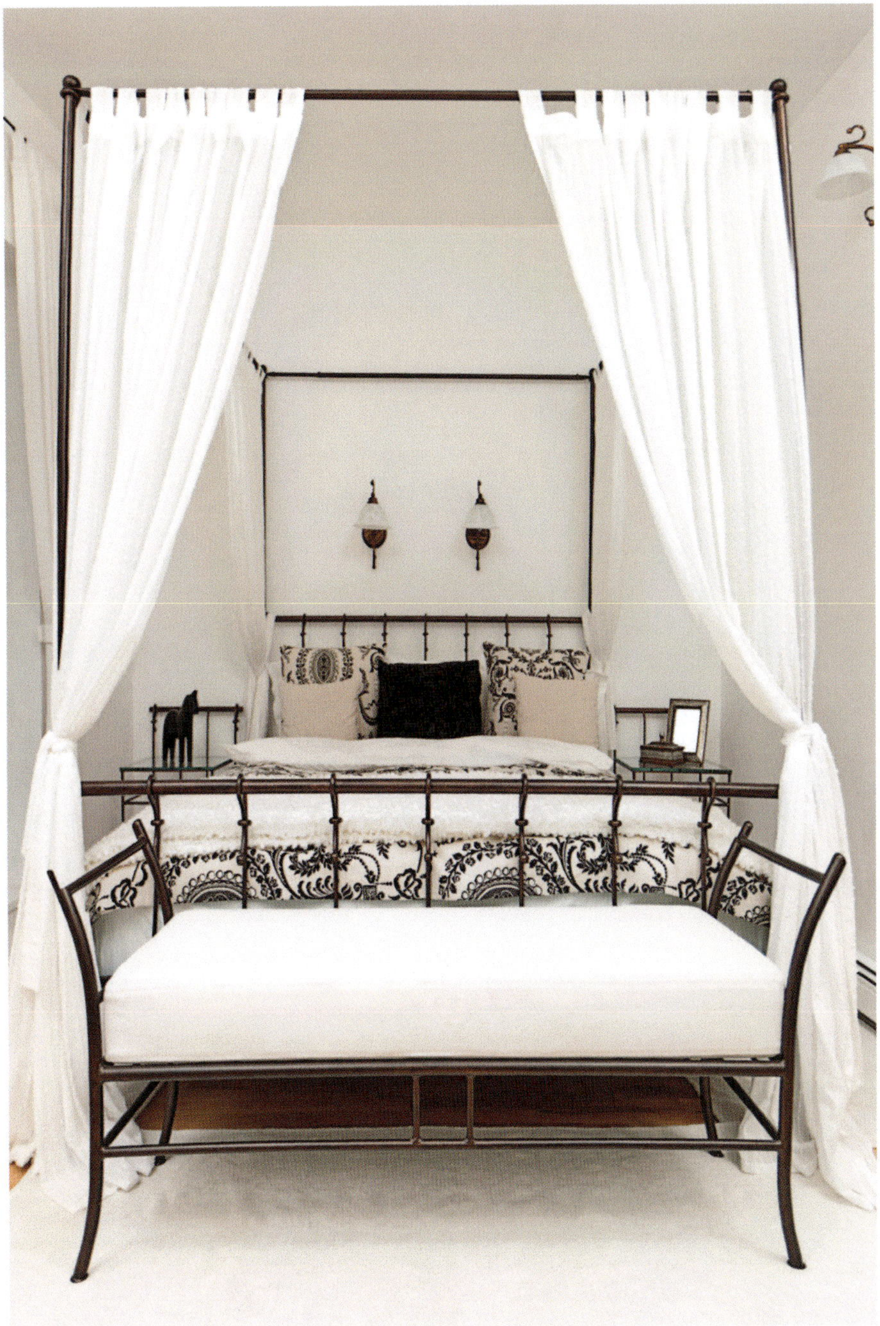

Old clock faces are very effective as wall decorations with an underlying symbolic or you can find interesting prints depicting a clock face.

Black And White Eternity

Black and white also lend themselves perfectly to an abstract idea that has an underlying symbolism, such as timelessness. For example: A collection of old clock faces, all different in their forms, but all connected through their black and white dials. These can be found at your local flea-markets. Such a collection makes a great wall decoration, especially if you arrange them together so that their different shapes and styles become apparent. Such a display immediately gives the room impact and interest.

You can then add a symbolic meaning to the collection, associating them with some special phrase or quotation. Clocks can remind us to take some restful time, set time apart for contemplation, and add more happy moments to life. There are so many attractive quotations around time that it is easy to find ones that have a special and personal meaning.

Other possibilities for creating this timeless rhythm could be to use a collection of letters in various sizes. They look great as a wall decoration, whether randomly combined or formed into words or sentences. Or just work with a mix-match of basic geometrical forms in pictures, bed linen and other textiles.

These are great ways of creating an attractive décor and adding symbolism which can have a very special meaning to you while it works positively on your subconscious mind. The idea can be interpreted in many ways, according to your special interest. Ideally, you want to margin it down to one special theme. The small bedroom will gain an allure of exclusivity that certainly will not cost as much as the impressive, stylish flair that you have produced.

*Work with a mix-match
of basic geometrical forms
in pictures, bed linen and other textiles
to create a sense of timelessness.*

Gray and white look very elegant, particularly when stripes are used.

Gray And Off-White Give An Exclusive Touch

Pale gray combined with lots of off-white is a great way to create an exclusive look for a small bed room. These hues will create a light transparency in the room which can be augmented by using glass or plexi-glass for the furniture. A pale gray for the walls, combined with white for the doors and window frames, will not only add a touch of superb elegance to the room, but will also give a sense of space.

The feel for such a room could be lightness, transparency, minimalism, calmness. An added theme could be placing the luxurious with simplicity. Pale gray is a neutral color and it enhances structures and surfaces beautifully: shimmering, silky textiles look superb when combined with rough linen; placing an exquisite silver vase full of white roses next to some decorative stones; a mother of pearl shell placed on an old pewter dish.

A rhythm of gray and white can be repeated throughout the small bedroom. Bed linen can be in off-white with gray trimmings or the other way round, gray with white accents. Textiles with plaids, stripes or florals look extremely refined when kept in gray and off-white. Because gray is very relaxing for the eye and neutral in its appearance, mixing and matching patterns will never be overwhelming in this color scheme.

Wall decoration can continue on the theme of transparency and lightness: pictures of sailing boats with their white sails against a gray horizon of the ocean and sky in the early morning; photos of beautiful white doves in flight, looking like ballet dancers. There are endless themes that express a sense of effortless movement and transparency in this color scheme, and can be chosen according to your own interests.

This color scheme is extremely versatile, and will lend itself beautifully to a romantic theme, minimal expression or a country look. Whatever style is desired, gray and off-white combinations and contrasting elements will always lead to an extremely elegant refinement, adding great style to your small bed room.

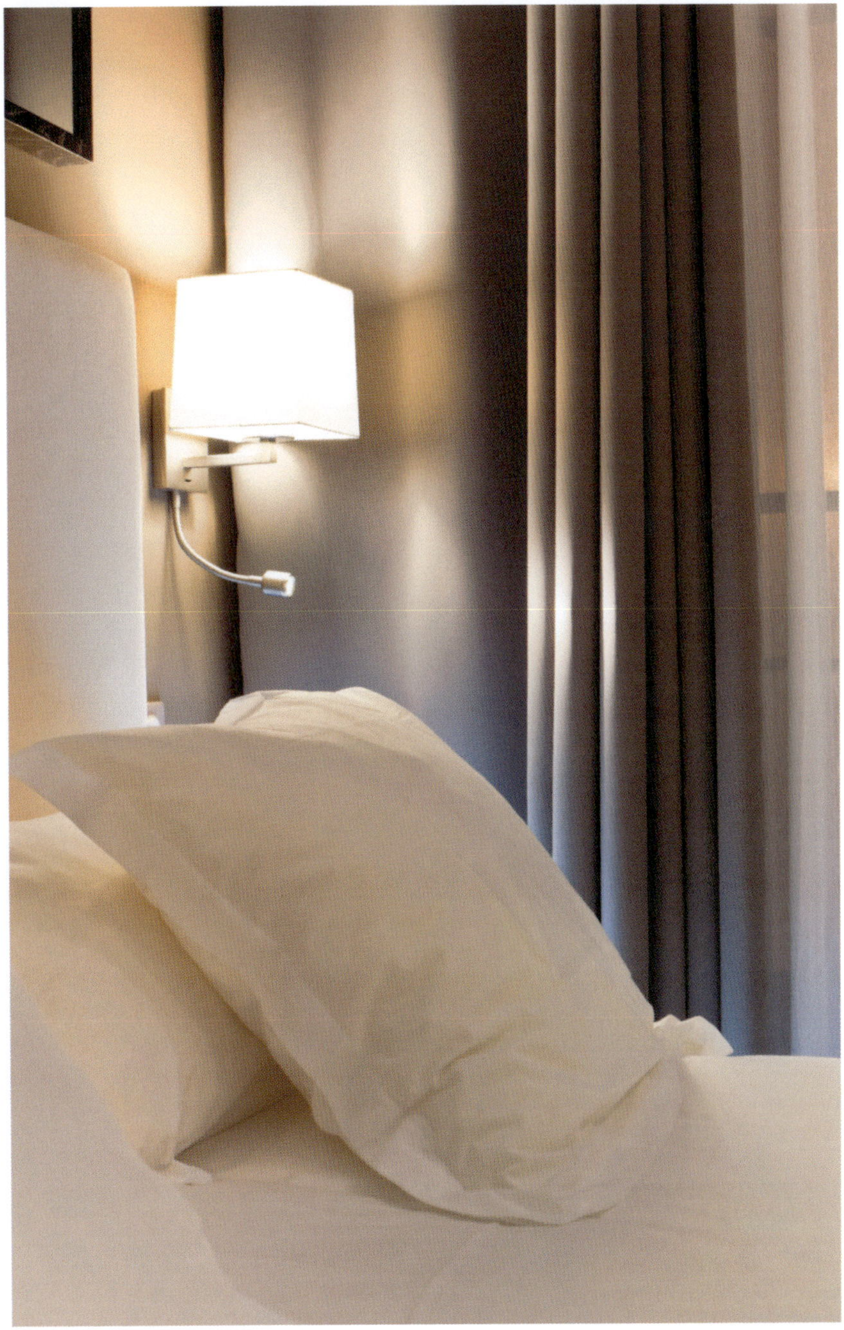

This is a lovely example of using a very pale shade of gray. A few accents of pure white enlighten the calming feeling. The interior designer, Kai Sunda, makes this small bedroom appear very spacious by adding accessories and furniture that imply space and movement.

The wall cabinets are placed asymmetrically and give the impression of movement, lightness and continuity. Lots of space is left around the pictures. The bed seems extremely light weighted because the support mechanism is not visible. The few colorful accents emphasize the spaciousness of this small bed-room.

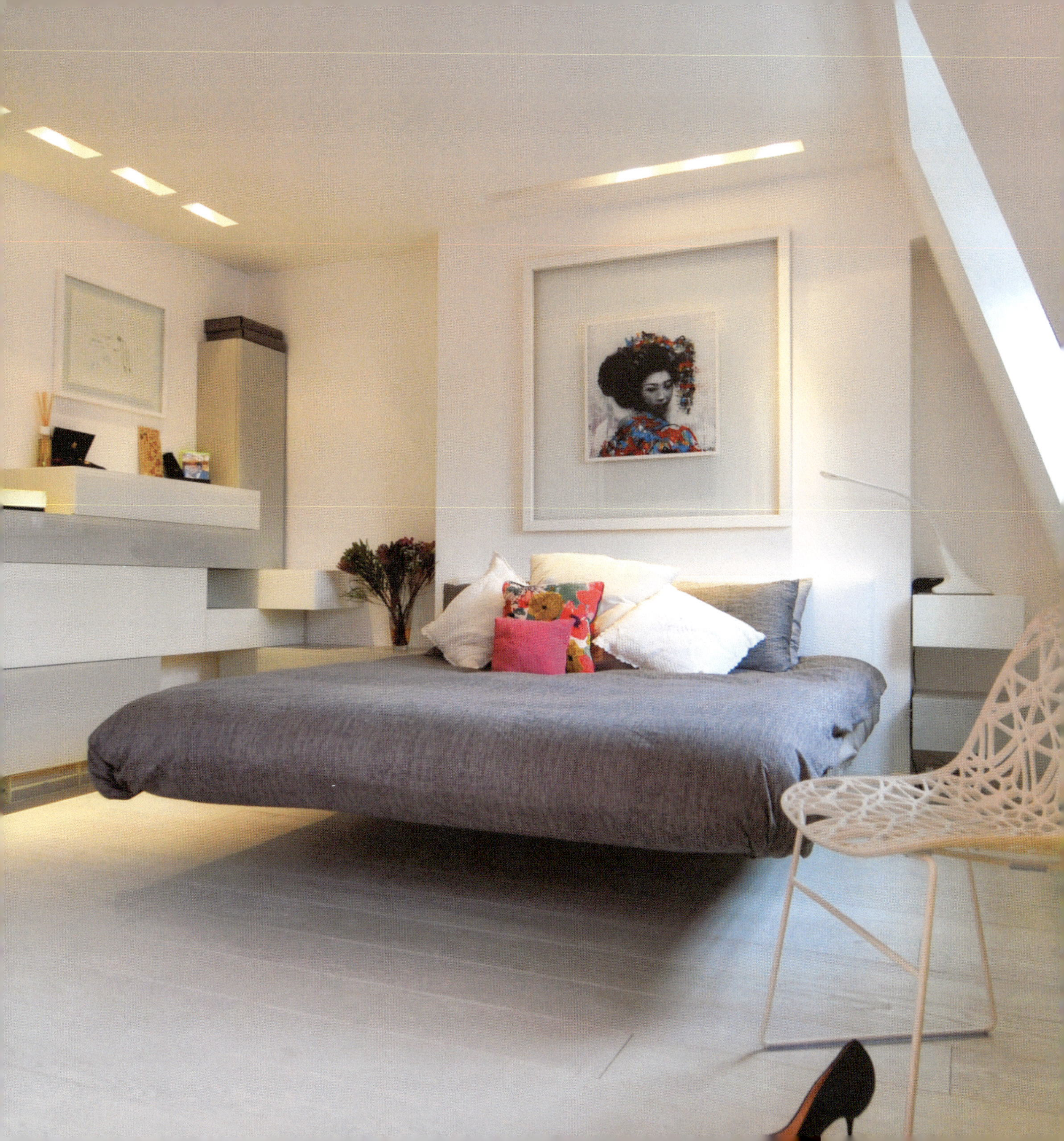

Blues
For
The
Small
Bedroom

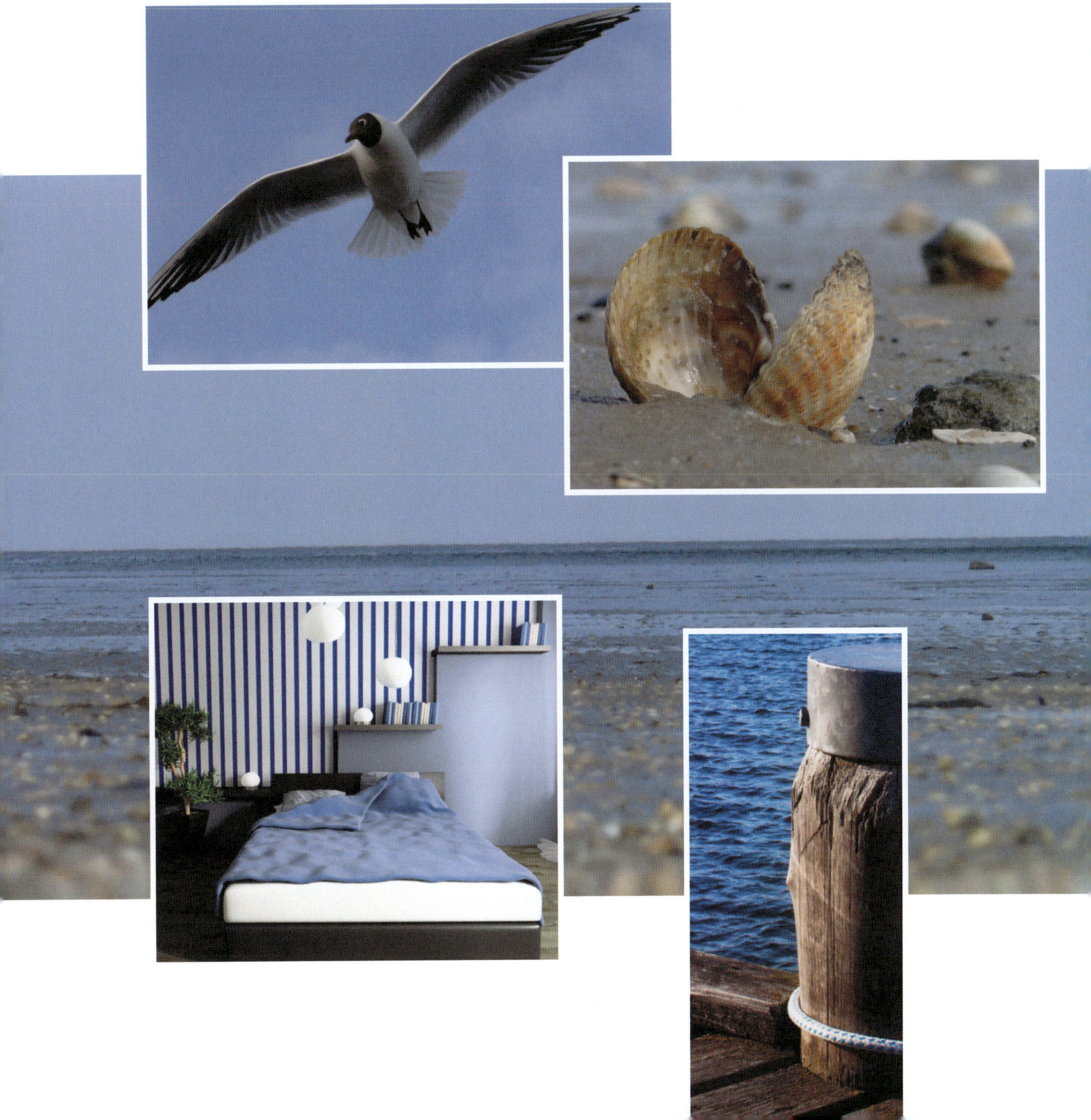

58 | *Contrasting a crisp blue with white creates a dynamic expression.*

Danish Design And Blue Add Spaciousness To The Small Bedroom

Danish style is ideal for a small bedroom and a very good way of adding a touch of class to this area. Typical colors of Danish design are pale blues, crème and natural tones of wood. These are excellent colors for making rooms look more spacious. The warm nuances of wood counteract the cooler blues and prevent the room from appearing too cold. The Danish simplicity of design in their furniture is excellent for using in a small bedroom.

When looking for ideas to create an interesting appearance for small bedrooms, look to see if they will adapt successfully to a small concept. This way you become far more creative and widen your perspective as to possibilities. This also helps to see the space objectively and not as a restricted and difficult area to design.

Ideally, the walls should be painted in a pale grayish blue, the ceiling and doors in a crème white. Pure white would make the blue appear too cool. Textiles are also kept in pale blue in order to create a sense of unity in the total appearance and retain the spacious effect. Pale blue always opens up space, like the early morning sky on the horizon of a pale, bluish gray ocean, giving an impression of infinity.

The Danish simplicity of design in their furniture will look great set against the soft blue walls. It helps to define the space, yet without cluttering it up. If the furniture is made of wood, it should be kept in a pale, light shade so that it does not appear heavy in a small bedroom. It also looks great set against a blue background. This combination creates an uncomplicated and amiable elegance.

Light plays an important role in Danish design. In fact, the natural light of Denmark is something very unique. It is this special, atmospheric northern light that has had decisive influence on Danish designers. It is no coincidence that some of the greatest lamp designers came from Denmark. In addition to being functional, their lamps are at the same time like small sculptures. Their clear designs make them excellent for a small bedroom. They create atmosphere and add a subtle artistic touch to a room without taking up precious space.

Every detail counts in the limited space of a small bedroom. By keeping to a basic color scheme and clear designs, as inspired by the Scandinavian natural colors, it is possible to give even a very small bedroom a classy touch. It makes the bedroom look far more spacious, but does not stretch a limited budget.

|61

An exclusive wardrobe is easy to construct by using panels of material and fixing a trailer to the ceiling. Every detail counts in Danish design, including the breakfast and porcelain.

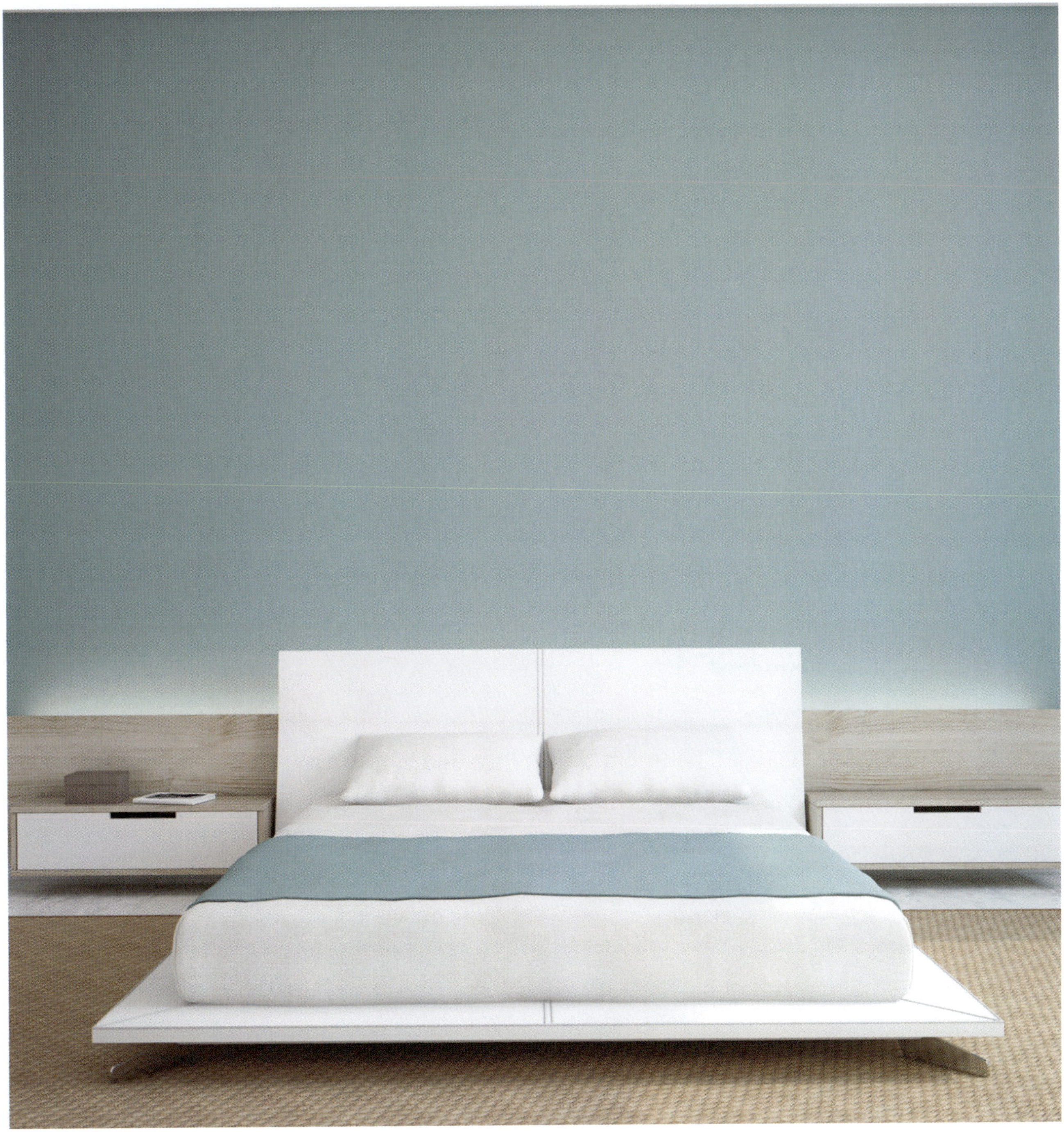

Maritime Blue Enchants The Small Bedroom

As previously mentioned, giving a room a theme, in addition to a color scheme, adds more expression and originality. Blue immediately lets you think of a maritime theme. This is in fact a very pleasant idea for a bedroom. It reminds one of those relaxing vacations and can help you to calm down. Such a positive depiction will also help you to wake up in a good mood. The small room leaves very little space for too many accessories. In such a small area, it is nevertheless easy to let the theme be well expressed.

A color scheme that not only includes blue but also soft sandy shades and the rich tones of wood will match the maritime scheme beautifully. The warm accents will add a friendly touch to the room.

For a romantic interpretation of the maritime theme, the old wooden ships of the 19th century are an excellent source for ideas. A wooden floor and furniture made of mahogany or oak would look great in contrast to blue walls or tone in tone against a sandy beige.

Bed clothes made of pure linen, in a natural hue combined with white, or white and blue, would be just fine for this theme. Wall pictures or photos disclosing oceanic scenes would round up the subject. This would be an ideal opportunity to display photos you have taken yourself during a seaside vacation and that have a very special meaning to you.

Another would be to give the theme a modern interpretation. Again, you could paint the walls blue, pale if you want the room to look larger, the darker blue shades to make it more intimate. The bedclothes with blue and white stripes would give that crisp energy we associate with the seashore. Pictures of modern, dynamic sailing boats would create a great feeling of space and movement as the boats sail through waves with grace and ease.

There are endless possibilities for interpreting this theme. With the appropriate color scheme, and well-chosen accessories, it is easy to make the maritime theme apparent the moment you enter the room and with this creating a charming, uplifting atmosphere.

Mahogany wood harmonizes beautifully with blue. A collection of wooden items from old boats is ideal for creating a maritime atmosphere.

|67

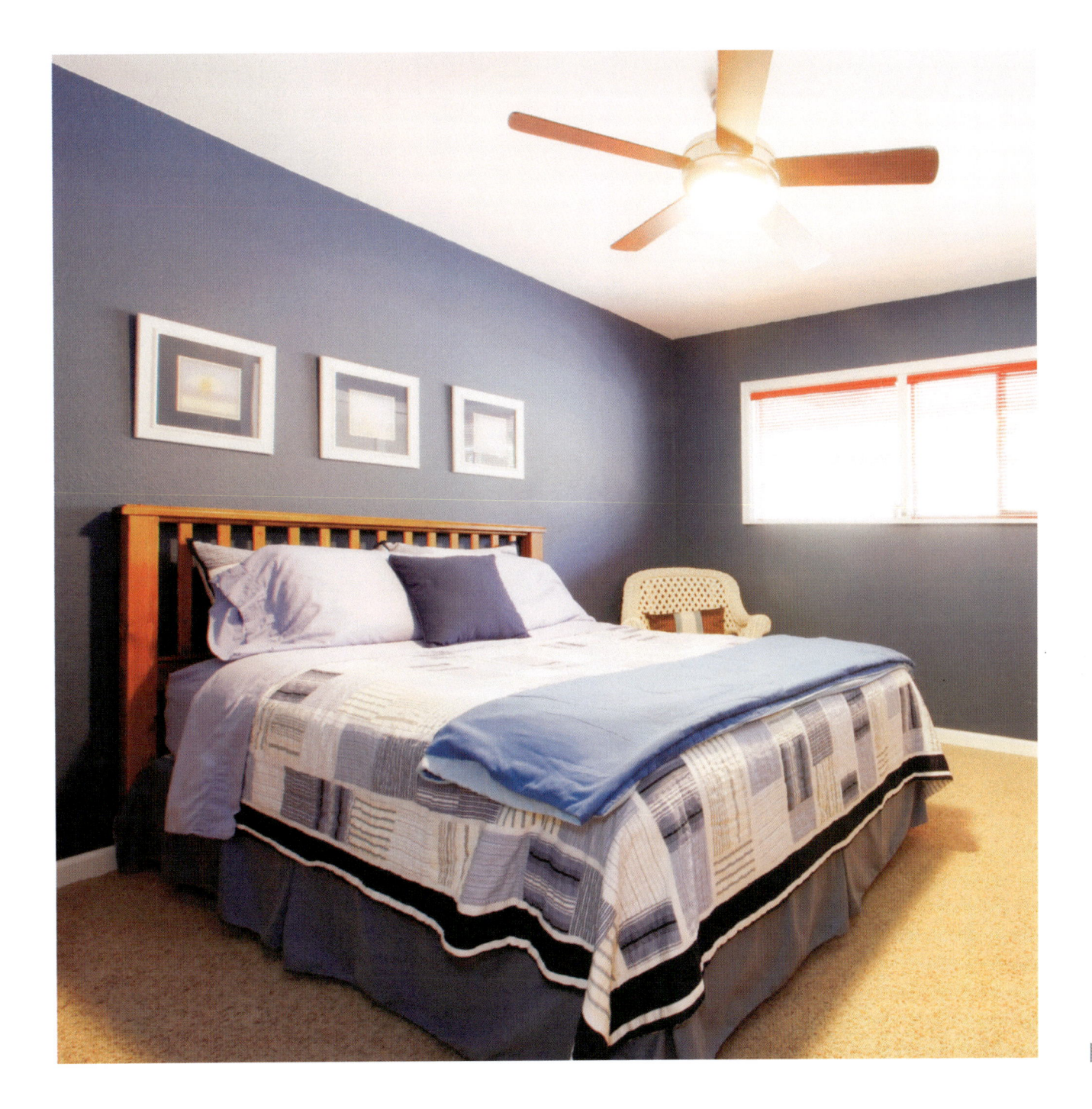

A very small room can gain considerable impact by choosing a theme, in this case, maritime. By including the color of the wall in the bed linen and in the curtains, the smallest room will gain vigor and flair.

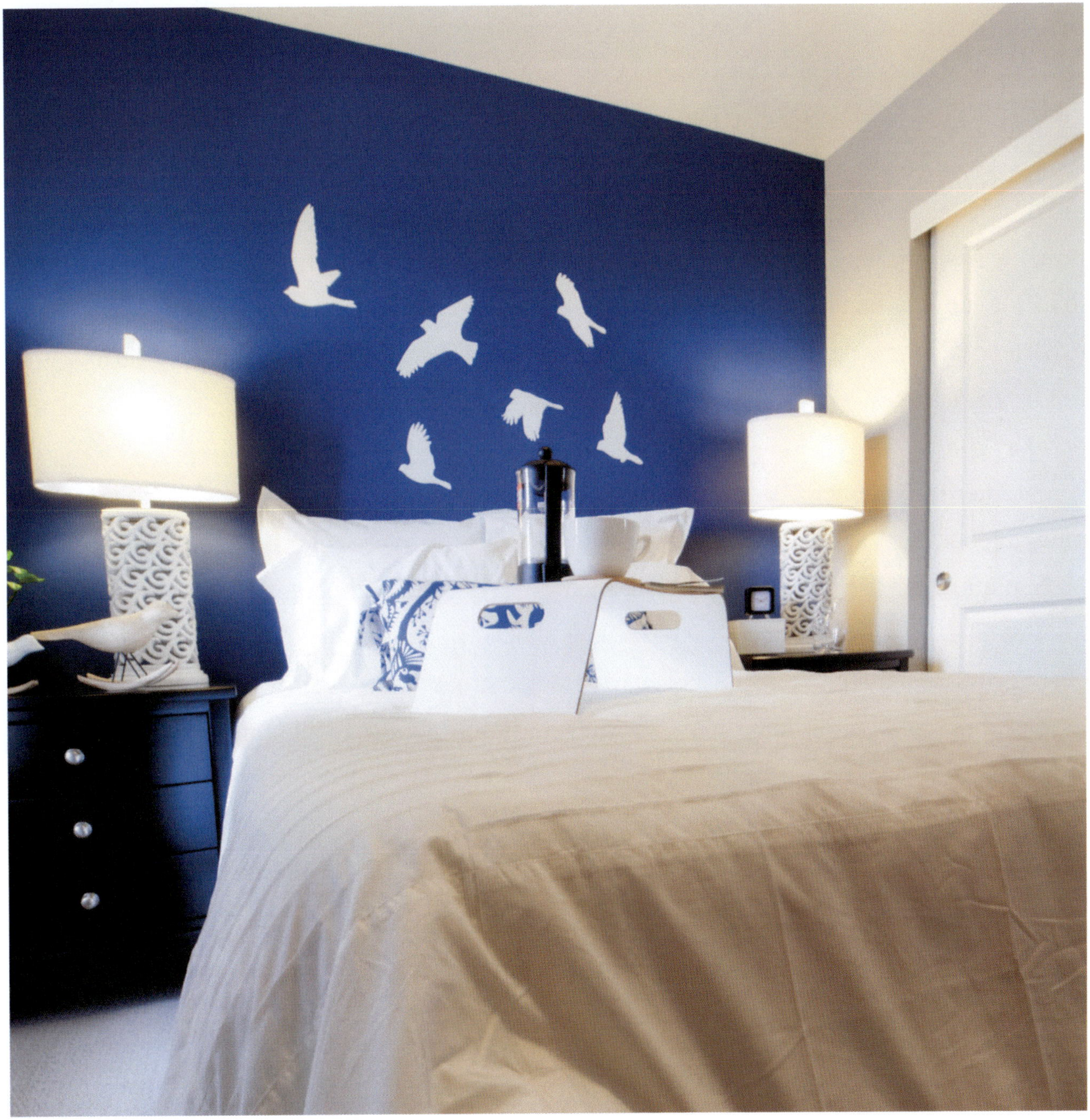

Monochromatic Harmonies

We talk about monochromatic harmonies when a color scheme is based on one hue only. Every color has a whole family of different shades, which are varied in value and saturation. By basing your color design for a small bedroom on one hue and applying all the possibilities for combinations, it is very easy to create attractive rooms, even if you are not very experienced. For large areas such a color scheme can tend to be monotonous, but certainly not in a small area.

There are many ways of combining the various shades. For example, a strong primal blue can look very dynamic when combined with white. A more colorful quality is obtained by combining the various shades of blue, such as turquoise, azure blue and a warm forget-me-not blue. Stripes and checks in the various shades of blue create another expression. So even if you are limited to this one group of colors, there is certainly no limitation to the possibilities for creating beautiful rooms. The same naturally applies to all other hues.

|71

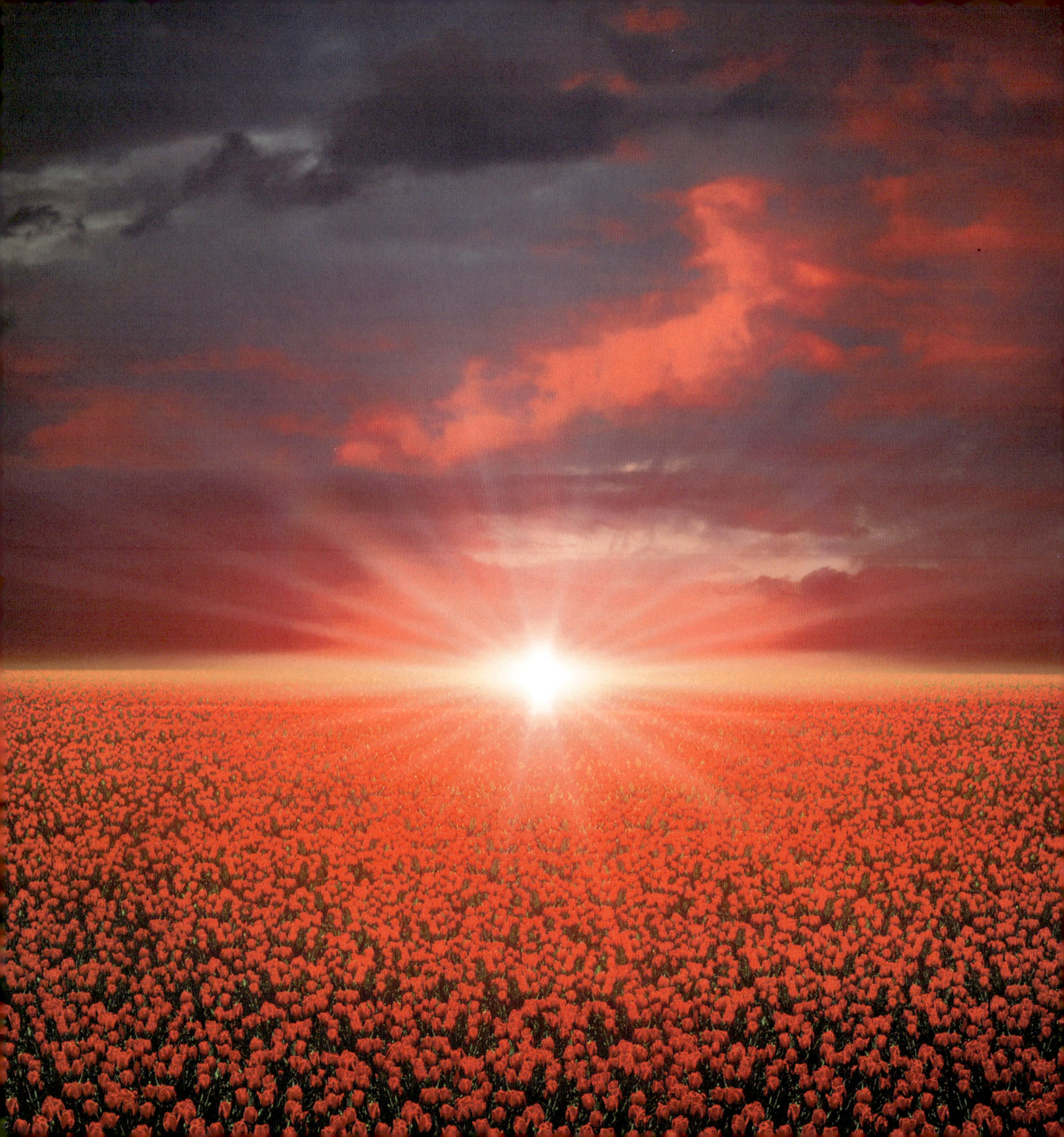

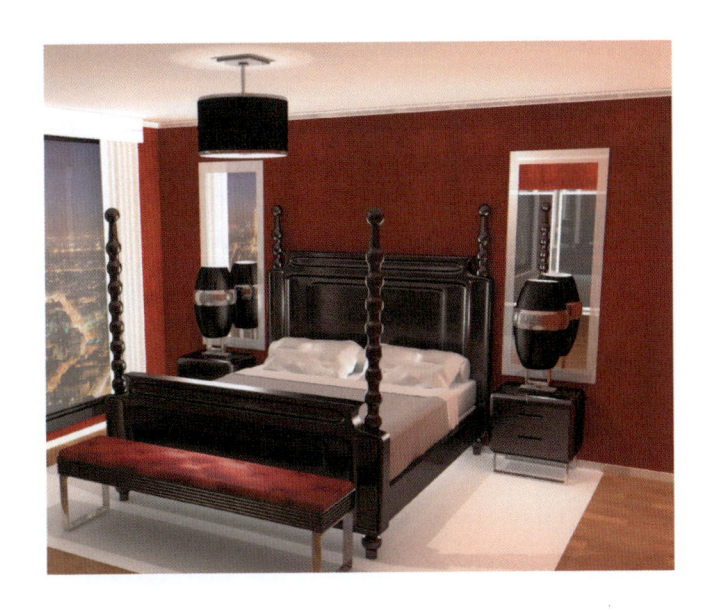

Bold Energy Colors

Dark Red Adds A Striking Elegance To The Small Room

Red is a most impressive color for a small room. Pure red would be too aggressive, but a darker shade, such as wine red, can add extreme elegance to even the smallest room. It will make the room seem darker but, at the same time, make it appear warmer and give it a touch of glamor. The neutrals that will be used in combination with wine red should be kept plain and simple, so that the small room does not appear cluttered. A neutral beige and accents of black would be excellent as a combination with this exclusive shade of red. It looks crisp and dominant in combination with white. The warm and rich quality of wine red will be augmented when combined with glowing shades of wood.

A question arises when using red for small rooms. Is red too aggressive for a small room? When a little black is added to red, it quietens the color down. This is particularly important for orange red which, in its full saturation, is an extremely agitating color. Once black is mixed in with red, the color becomes more earthy, more peaceful; it is on its way to becoming brown. Unlike brown, however, it still has the empowering characteristics of a pure red: it is far more dramatic and impacting. Both wine red and rusty red add a touch of luxury to even the smallest space.

If it feels too overwhelming to use wine red as a color for all the walls, you can still achieve a dramatic impact by painting only one wall in this hue, leaving the others in a cool beige or white, according to the chosen color scheme. This alone will add tremendous impact to the room. If the room is awkward in shape, red can help to change and improve this, either by adding dramatic accents and diverting the attention from ungainly space areas, or adding focus to the more attractive areas.

Light beige contrasts for the ceiling, doors and some of the linens, add softness to the strong wine red, and prevent the room from appearing too dark. A plain, light colored wooden floor, or beige woolen rugs, elegant bed linen in beige, would all add a refined elegance to wine red. Accessories in varnished glossy black will add the final touch of elegant glamor and reflect beautifully any surrounding light, be this from sunlight, lamps or candles.

A dark red adds warmth to a city bedroom. Combined with black, it gains distinction. When the dark red is combined with naturals, a homely country style is created.

77

Combine red with wood to create a really cozy atmosphere.

|79

Red is a great color if you just want to add a few imposing accents to create warmth and excitement in a quiet area. The interior designer, Kathryn Johnson, has turned a small nook into a beautiful, comfy and cozy area which is excellent as a guest room or as a special place to sit and read.

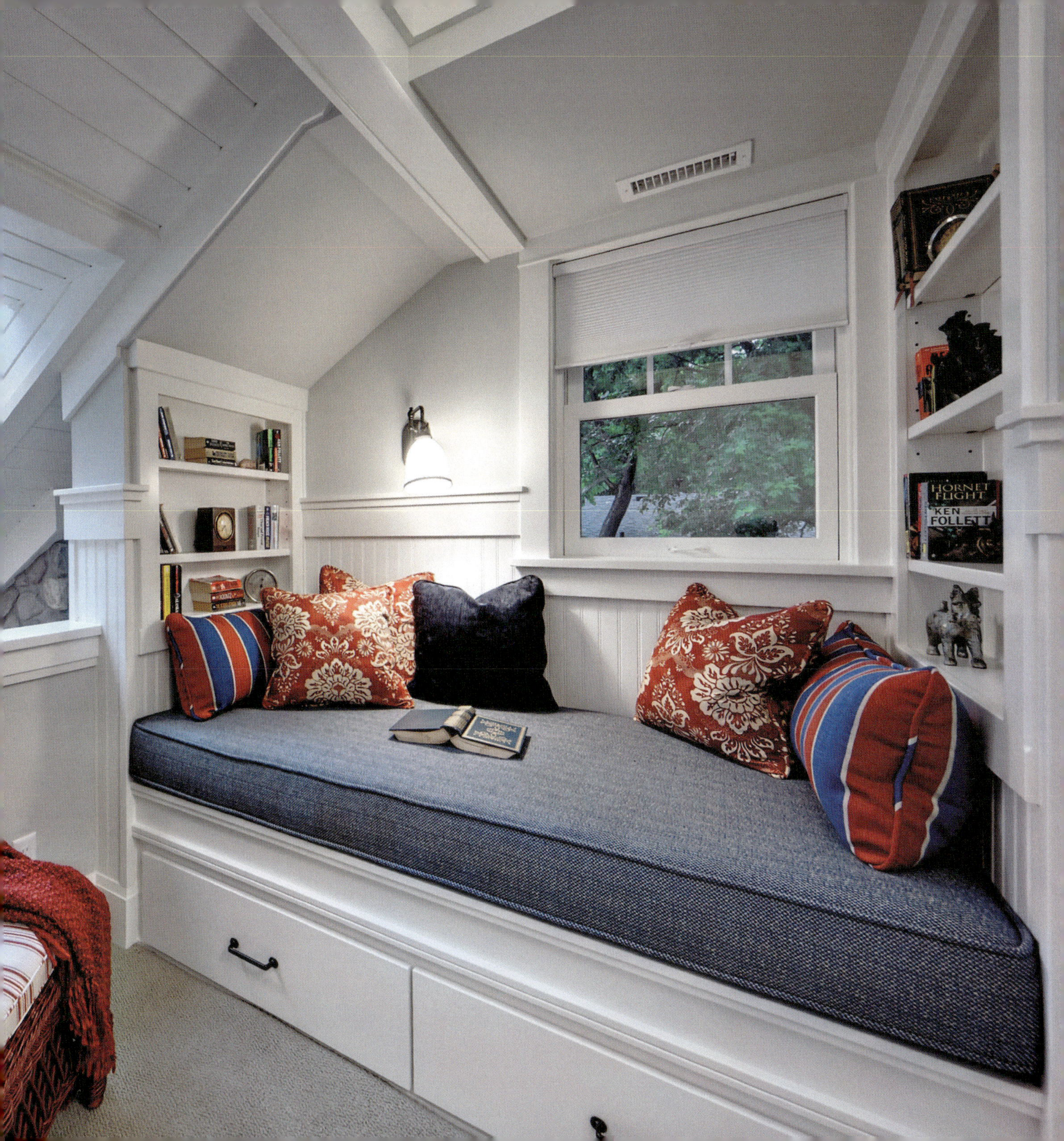
HORNET
FLIGHT
KEN
FOLLETT

Big and Bold With Orange

We often tend to think small when deciding on a color scheme and furniture for a small bedroom. Sometimes, however, the space can be really so small that the opposite way of thinking would be the solution, and even result in a very attractive and snug bedroom. The bed could take up, more or less, nearly all the space. There are some great Japanese styled beds that have a projecting frame surrounding them. This projection is excellent for placing lamps and other items, such as books and your breakfast coffee pot. Or you can install night tables and shelves which look neater and take up less space.

Bold colors can give the space energy. One of the most popular colors for rooms is the good-natured and energetic orange. It is a mixture of yellow which is symbolic for the intellect, and of red symbolizing emotionality. Orange has its very own characteristic. It connects the intellect and strong emotionality to become a good natured color. It does not have the aggressiveness of red, but shares its energy. It is not as intellectual as yellow, but sheds the same brightness and joy.

It is certainly an excellent hue to brighten up a room and give it a warm and generous feeling. It creates a cheerful, expressive setting. Used in full saturation, it can be over stimulating and too boisterous. Therefore, care needs to be taken when using this color for walls. It may need mellowing down a little, especially when all the room is being painted in this hue.

One big picture with a clear statement would also look amazingly good in a small space. There is not much space to move around in such a small room, but you will certainly not feel you are entering a stifling area. On the contrary, it will give you a feeling of generosity and openness.

Neighboring Colors Like Each Other

Colors that are next to each other on the color wheel are easy to combine for a small bedroom, especially for the less experienced. Because each hue has a family of various shades, the variations for attractive combinations are extremely versatile. You can paint a room in one shade and then add a large picture or bed-cover which includes the various shades of neighboring hues. This way you can create a beautiful room without risking expensive mistakes.

The examples of the neighboring yellow, orange and red show various ways of combining these hues for attractive results. Some show the combination of primal colors, others show the results that can be achieved when using muted shades of the same hues.

There are various neighboring color schemes within the color wheel such as: turquoise, green and lemon green; blue, purple and magenta; purple, red and orange. As mentioned, you need to pay attention to the various shades of each hue. The muted hues are preferred for bedrooms.

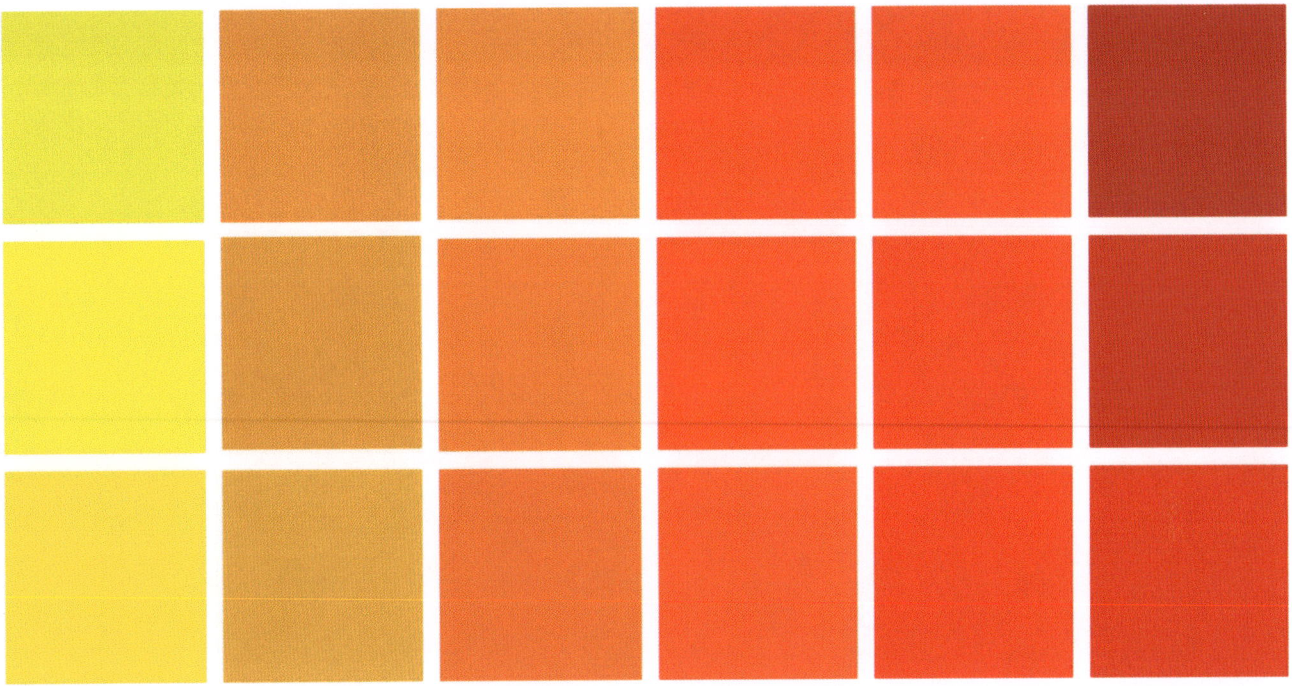

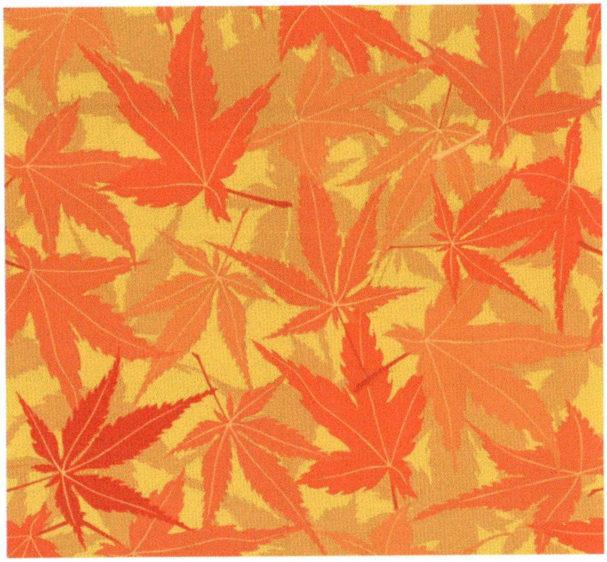

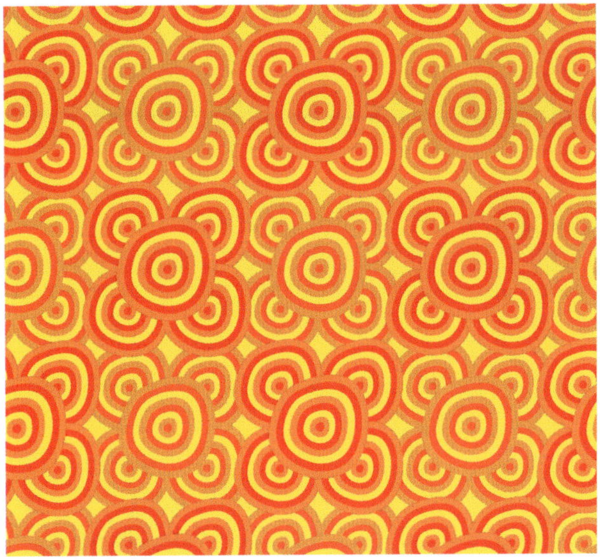

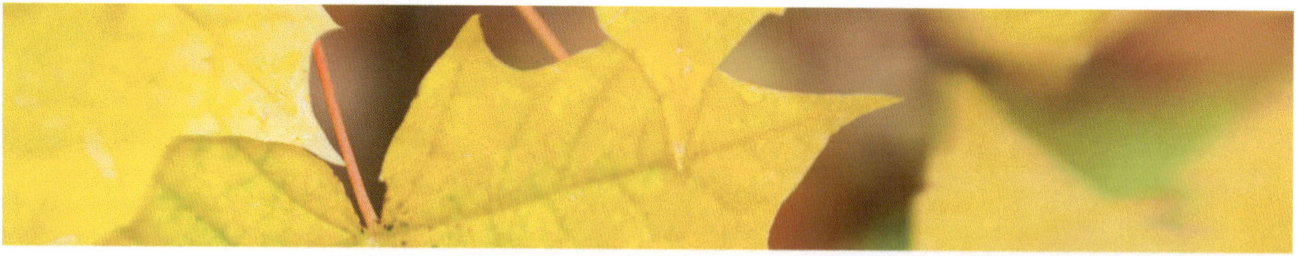
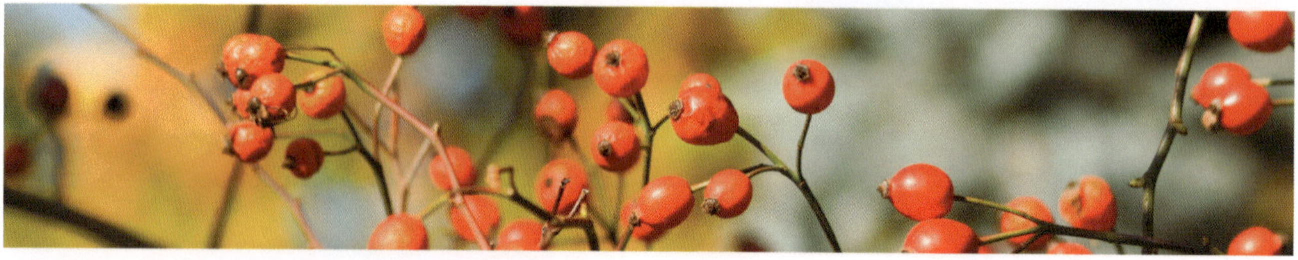
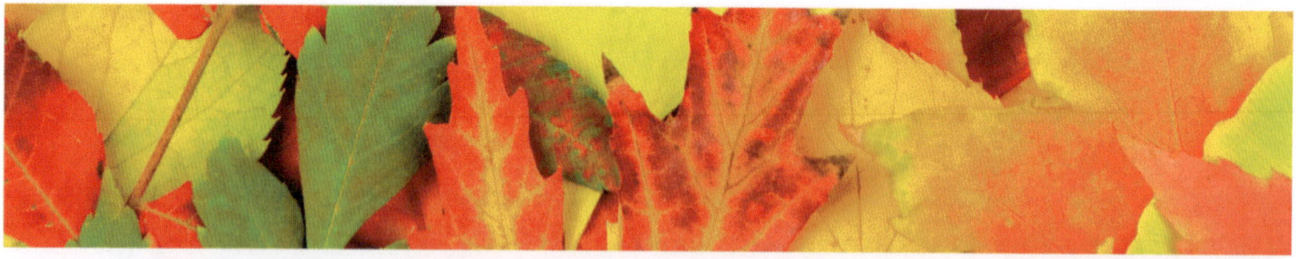
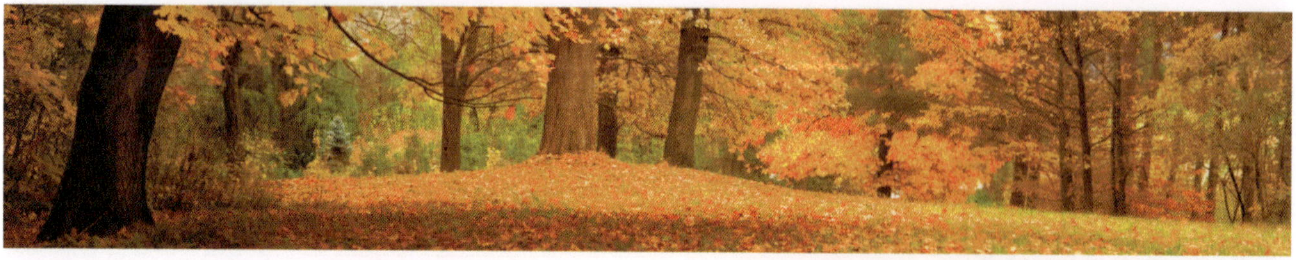
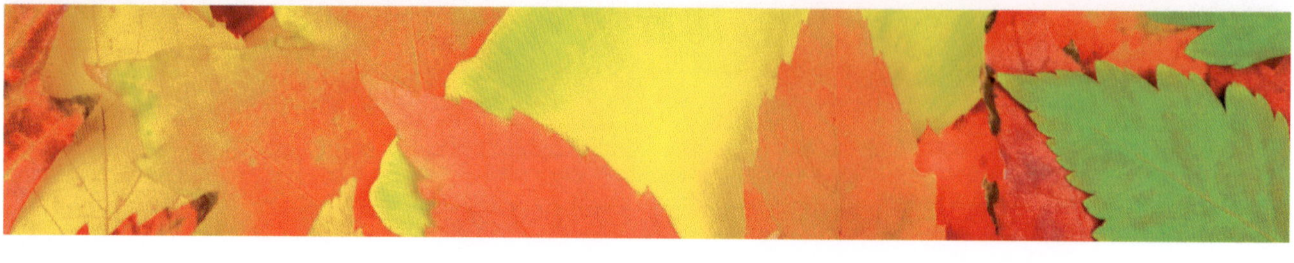

Orange Portrays All Of The Gorgeous Warm Tones Of Autumn

The splendor of autumnal orange tones enliven any room, beautifying it and making it look most inviting. During autumn we experience the softer tones of orange in a most beautiful array of shades. Naturally, we want to imitate this amazingly impressive arrangement of warm hues in our living areas. As mentioned, orange itself can overpower, but since it varies from warm beige, apricot, to russets and golden browns, it is easy to find the exact hue and brightness to suit the room.

A possible idea is to use the soft neutral beige tones, then add accents of bold orange. This gives the impression of warmth and high energy but at the same avoids having an orange room that is too dominant and aggressive. If you love lots of colors, then naturally the splendid oranges and russets of autumn offer superb ideas for color schemes to reproduce in your rooms making them glow with these gorgeous colorings.

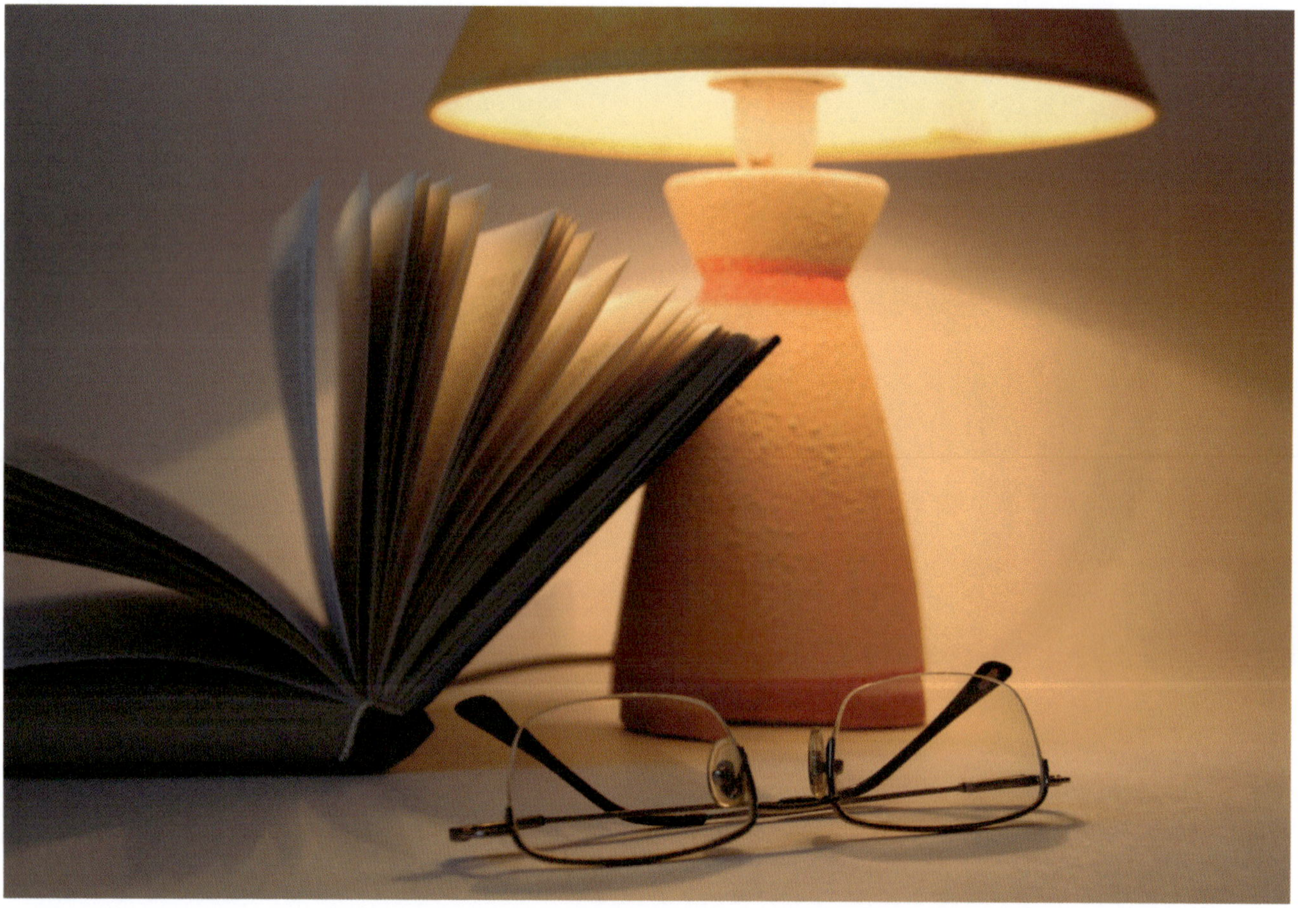

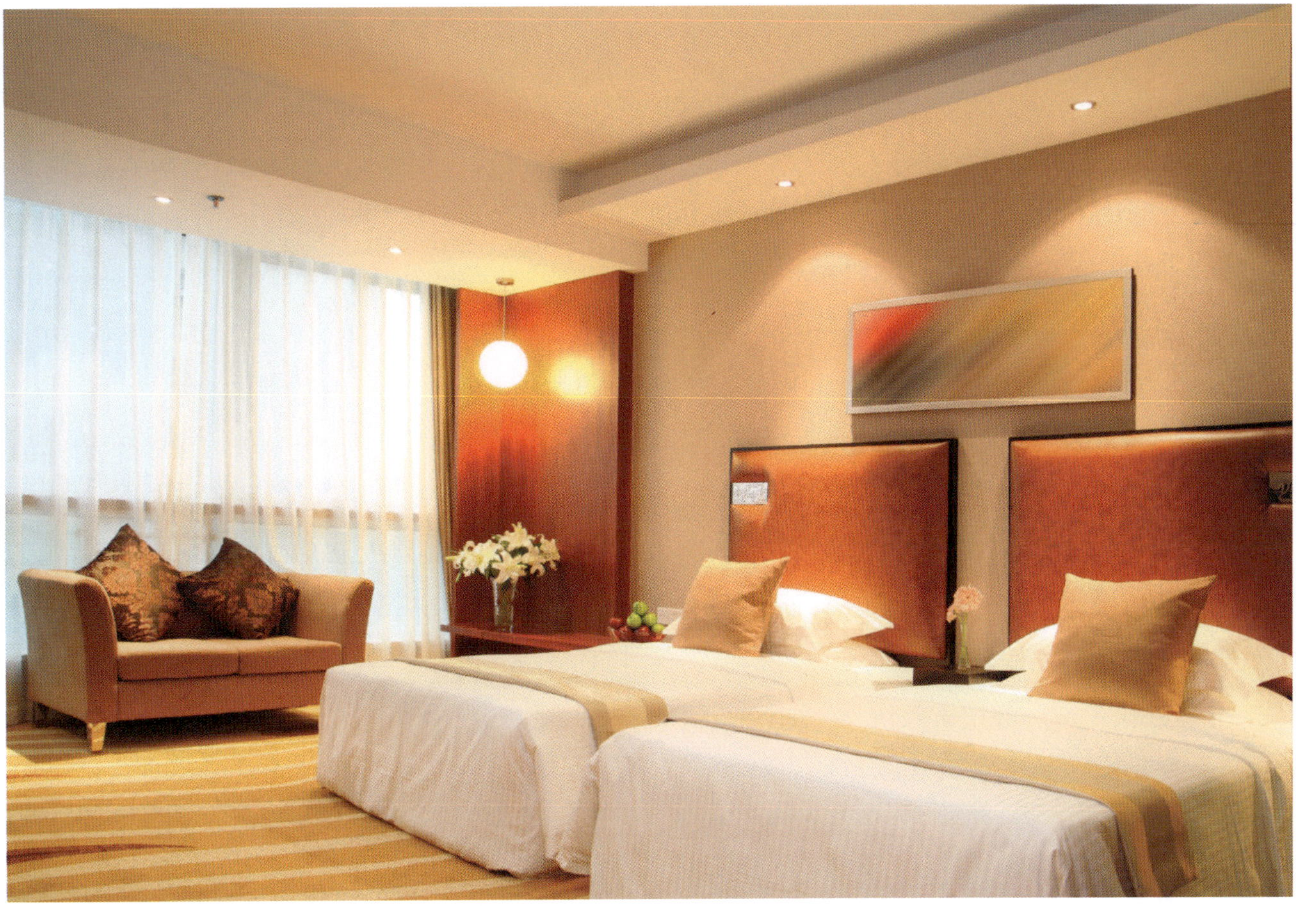

As autumn departs to make room for winter, it leaves us with the beautiful refined hues derived from orange: warm beiges leaning towards apricot, russet reds and dark browns.

The interior designer, Charmean Neithart, has taken the neutral tones of the orange family, to convert a small guest room into a charming, refuge, basing her color scheme on the neutrals of the orange family.

A duvet made of ikat fabric and accessories give a subtle ethnic theme to the room.

|91

The Dramatic Energy Of A Museum

Some marvelous designs for murals have come onto the market, which can add such a beautiful energy to your small bedroom. Murals have attracted the attention of many famous architects, artists and sculptures and they have created some extremely interesting designs for wall coverings. These can be purchased from many producers of fine wallpapers.

Murals are great for adding one strong, impacting statement to a small bedroom. They are available to suit every style. For those who love lots of color, you will find many designs, which are a bit outrageous in the use of color, but always excellent in style. Some of the designs have enormous depth thanks to the interplay of organic shapes, dynamic lines, shimmering metallic, and contrasts of bright and dull areas. These are excellent for opening up space and giving the impression that the room is larger. Others use geometry as the theme for their design.

These murals are a superb way of adding impact to a small bedroom. It is important that the bed linen and accessories are matched in color and style to those in the mural. This will prevent the small room from being overwhelmed with too much visual information. In fact, the small room would look great if nothing more than a bed and lighting were added. This way, the mural would remain the center of attraction. It will create such an impacting atmosphere, which will totally redefine the small space, making it appear spacious and giving an over-dimensional artistic touch that you would normally only find in a museum. There is no reason not to give that small room a dash of museum superiority.

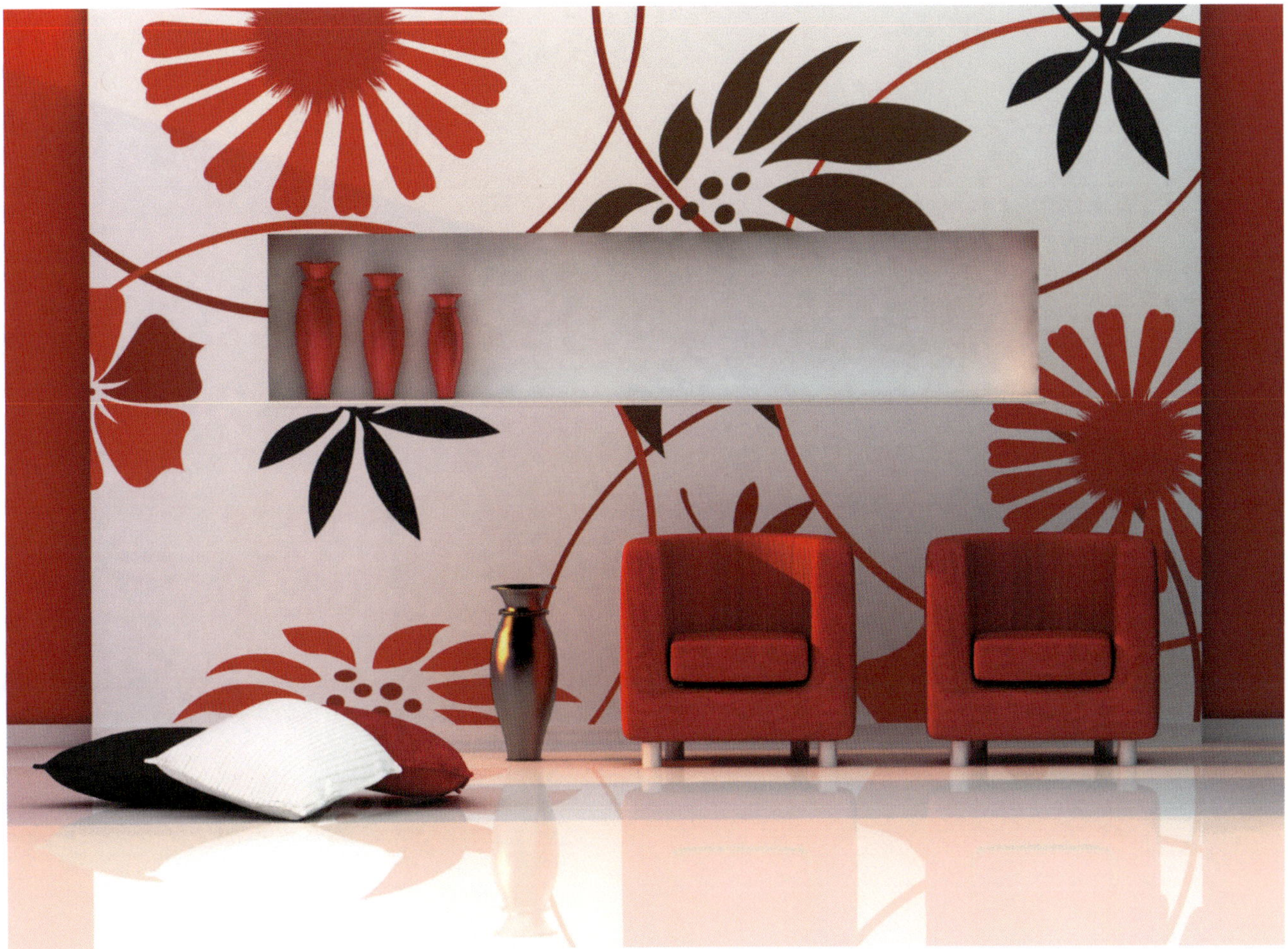

The designer, Neslihan Pekcan, adds the dramatic energy of a museum to this small bedroom and creates an impacting atmosphere which totally redefines the small room, giving it an esprit that transcends by far the confinements of the narrow space.

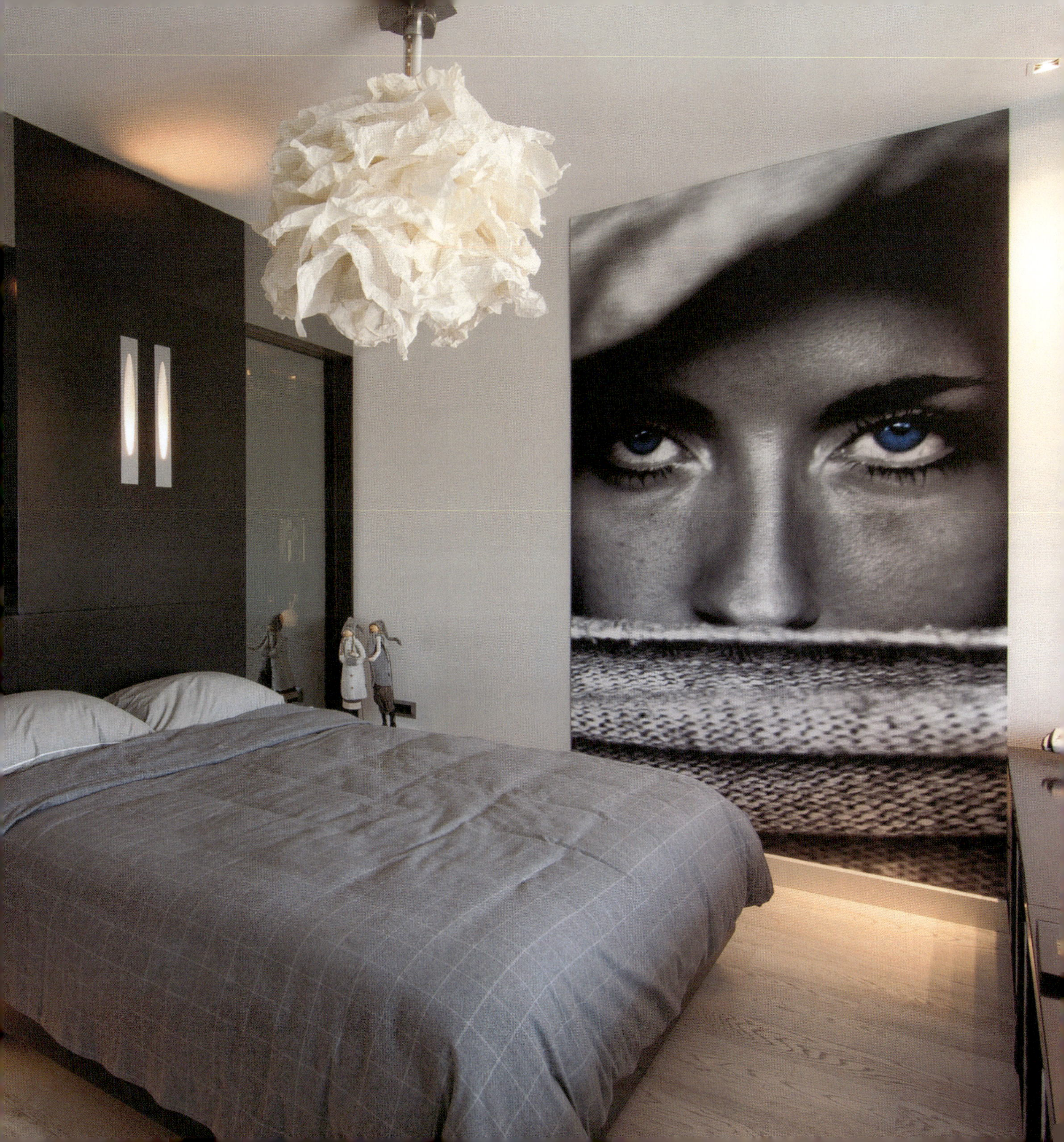

96 | *Large murals or pictures add a dramatic effect to a small bedroom.*

97

Complementary Colors Love Each Other: Red And Green

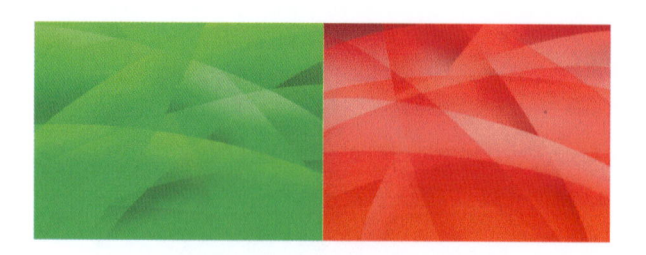

A complementary color scheme is excellent for creating an interesting and very attractive space without overwhelming the limited area of a small bedroom. This way you limit the use of color, but use them in different variations throughout the room design. Complementary colors harmonize so well, that you can be free to combine patterns, stripes, warm and cold, without the fear of making a mistake.

It is very easy to create a superb small bedroom by concentrating on one pair of complementary colors. Complementary colors consist of two hues that are opposite each other on the color wheel. An example would be red and green, which can easily be applied to a bedroom. Green adds serenity to a bedroom and red adds cheerful highlights.

In order to ensure that these complementary colors work well together, it is important to remember that green has a tendency to be passive. This is the reason it makes rooms appear calm. Red projects itself forward and appears even more lively in combination with green. In order to balance the colors, so that red does not overwhelm the room, it is advisable to use only accents of this hue.

Red and green complement each other really well: by adding white, the quality becomes more abstract but still very effective.

There are many textiles available, such as bed linen and curtains, which include both green and red in their pattern design. Artists love this color combination and have created great pictures using only red and green. Therefore, it is easy to apply this color scheme throughout the room.

There are various complementary pairs, such as blue and orange, purple and spring green or violet and yellow, which can be applied in the same way as the example of green and red. The advantage of staying within a complementary combination of two colors is that you can create a much stronger impact for a small bedroom or any other living space. This is an easy and affordable way to add a sparkling color effect to a small room without overwhelming it.

Both green and red have a lovely family of various light and dark hues, which are actually much better for decorating a small bedroom. Red has great shades of pale pinks and warm beige tones which look excellent combined with all nuances of green. These are not as overwhelming as the fully saturated red and can be used more liberally in combination with green.

Complementary red and green still harmonize beautifully even when they are darker, as wine red or lighter as a pale sage green. A dark green looks exquisite when combined with a warm pink that has been derived from red. In fact, when you are familiar with all the hues in each of these color families, the possibility for combinations is almost endless.

|101

Complementary Colors Love Each Other: Blue And Orange

Blue and orange are a gorgeous complementary pair and very popular in interior design. As with all complementary pairs, they are far more intensive when combined together. However, only a few accents of orange are required to add a joyous quality to the normally serene blue. Orange likes to steal the show and too much will cause the blue to disappear totally into the background. Just vivid accents of orange here and there are sufficient to create the energizing freshness and fiery energy of this pair of colors.

The excitement of creating a color scheme with complementary colors is that the system works even if you are designing with all of the shades of these colors. In the case of the complementary colors blue and orange, apricot – a paler shade of orange – looks great with a dusky blue. A warm beige, which belongs to the orange family, will harmonize perfectly with all shades of blue. Dark brown wood (dark brown is often achieved by adding black to orange), will look great with pale blue walls.

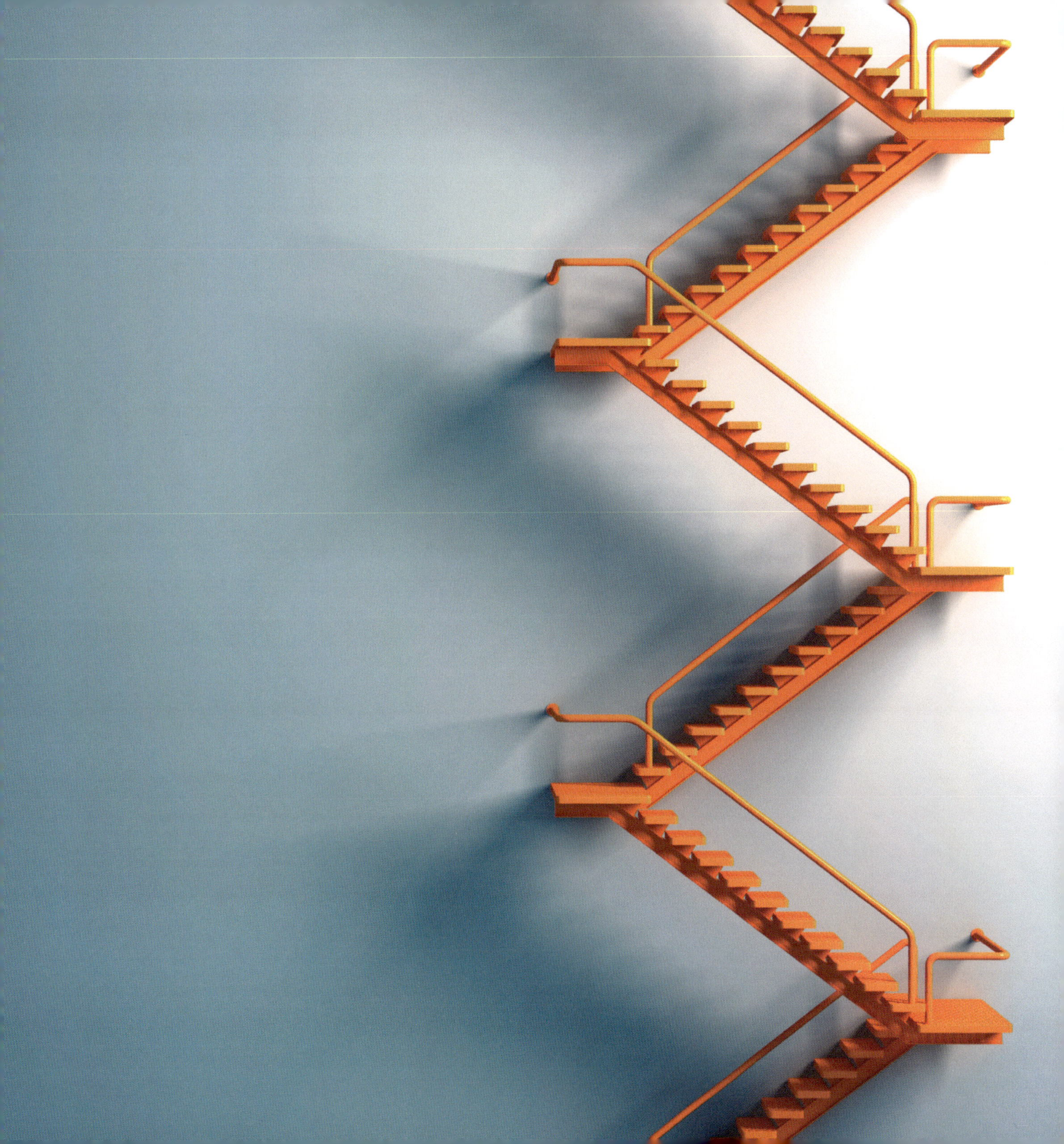

This beautiful pattern has been designed with a dark blue and various soft hues that have been derived from orange.

Apricot, and all neutral hues derived from orange look extremely attractive when combined with blue.

Complementary Colors Love Each Other: Purple And Yellow

In the northern countries, the first flowers to appear around Easter time are mainly yellow and purple. These are often crocuses or primroses.

Although purple and yellow appear to be very different, purple being the darkest color and yellow the lightest, they do actually have many things in common. In addition to being complementary, both colors represent the mind, violet the unconscious, yellow the conscious.

Because yellow is the lightest color and purple the darkest they create a bold contrast when combined. Since they represent abstract ideas, they are not very popular as colors for using in interior decorating. However, the softer hues of yellow and purple, such as cream and a grayed violet can add considerable distinction to an interior. Camel, derived from yellow, looks great with lilac, a pale bluish hue derived from purple.

Both colors have a large family of hues to choose from and since they are complementary these will always match up beautifully.

|107

108 | ***Soft shades of yellow combine perfectly with lighter hues of the purple family.***

Just as the primary colors, yellow and purple, combine beautifully, so do also the softer shades derived from these hues. The color scheme for this bedroom is based on a yellowish wood for the furniture, like that of sand dunes, and lighter shades of purple.

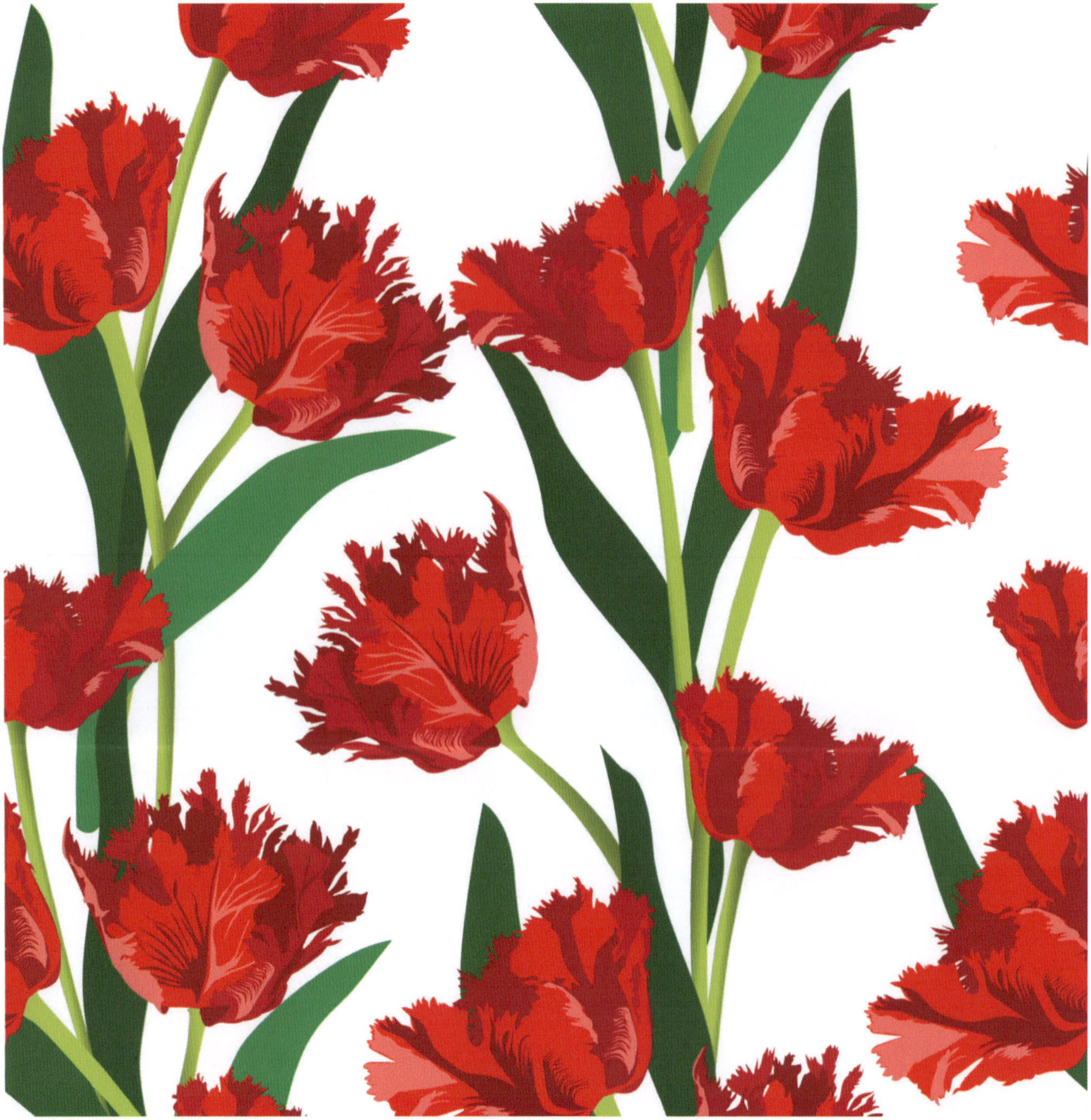

Swerving Tulips Add A Colorful Zest

In spring, the local parks are exploding with radiant pink, yellow, blue, orange and violet blossoms: flower power pure! You can adopt this impacting experience beautifully to a decoration for a small bedroom.

There are many gorgeous fabrics designed with swirling, dancing tulips. The optimistic, upward curving stems and colorful blossoms add a joyful highlight to a room. It is important to have lots of white space around the tulips. This will create a dimensional impression of space and adds flower power to the small room without being overwhelming.

Such a large pattern on textiles is excellent for making into straight panels for the windows or for enclosing a wardrobe space. When the panels are fixed into a ceiling trailer, they create a Japanese styled, sliding-door effect. The dynamic pattern would appear like a large mural. Alternatively, it would be possible to take one's own photos of tulips and enlarge them to make prints for walls.

Many companies offer variations of tulip patterns in bed linen, which creates a beautiful bed of flowers. Or, alternatively, the bed-linen could be kept in a single color to match one of the tulips. The idea of a flower theme easily adopts to almost any type of flowers. An extravagant quality is achieved by making them far bigger than their original size.

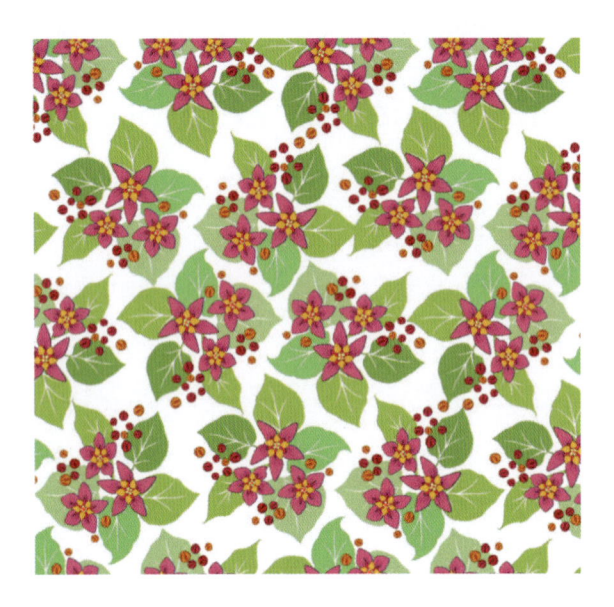

With Pink and Green It is Spring Time All Year Round

Spring is full of blossoms, and with solid consistency the cherry trees are covered with beautiful, fluffy, pink blossoms. The grass is a fresh, young green and tiny spring green leaves perk up the trees and bushes. Pink and purple tulips from Holland are crowded into buckets in front of the local florists, looking lavishly generous and full of that vibrant energy so typical for spring.

Although this scene repeats itself every year, it always seems so refreshingly new. Perhaps it seems so because it only lasts for such a short time. Fortunately, at least the color scheme can be kept spirited for a longer period. These are excellent colors for using to add a joyful lightness to a small bedroom.

Pink and spring green will transform a small, boring room into a bright space full of joy and fun. They emanate sheer optimism. Especially the stronger shades of purple pink, which give an extravagant touch to it, and make the room seem charmingly naive. They are naturally excellent colors for a young girl's room.

Using the softer shades of pink in combination with a muted, light green will create an entirely different energy. Like the exquisite cherry blossoms, the room will look dainty and demure. By using modern, sporty textiles, this will help this picturesque color scheme not to be too sweet. If care is taken to use a balance of green and pink in the textiles and accessories, a small room can look exceptionally elegant, somewhat reminiscent of times past, bringing old values back to life. Too much sweetness can be counteracted by using coarse linen, clear lines and limiting the small space to basic needs, avoiding clutter and too many decorative items.

It is always interesting to experience how even small rooms can be transformed into exceptional spaces when applying colors. Because purples and greens are so vast in the shades they offer, it is possible to create a great many imaginative and expressive variations of this color theme, all of which will certainly add vigor or charm to even the smallest bedroom.

Pink and green add a dash of freshness to this antique, intimate bedroom.

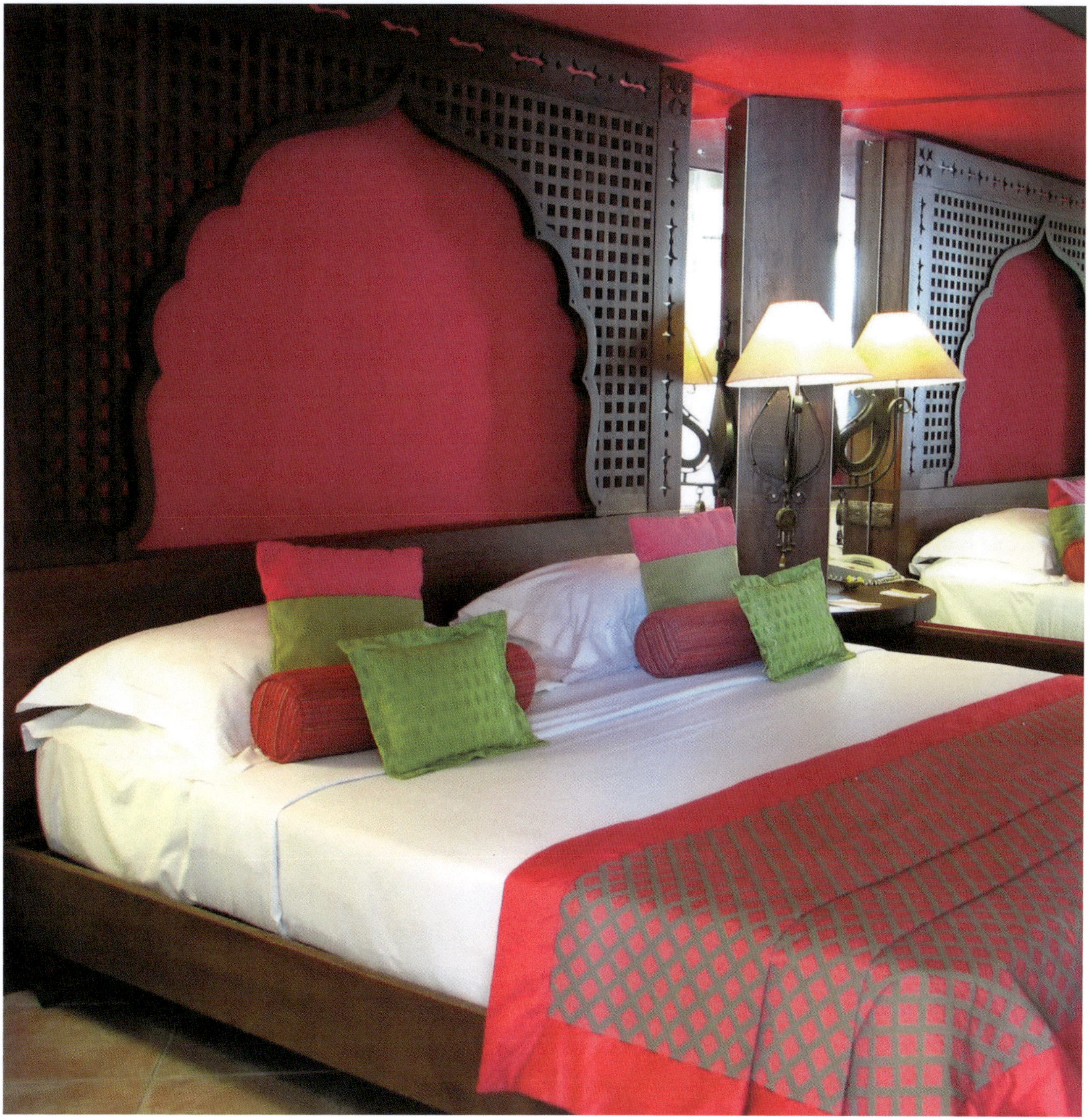

Moods Created By Color

245 FOWLER PINK

230 OINTMENT

ALAMINE

CINDER ROSE 246

202

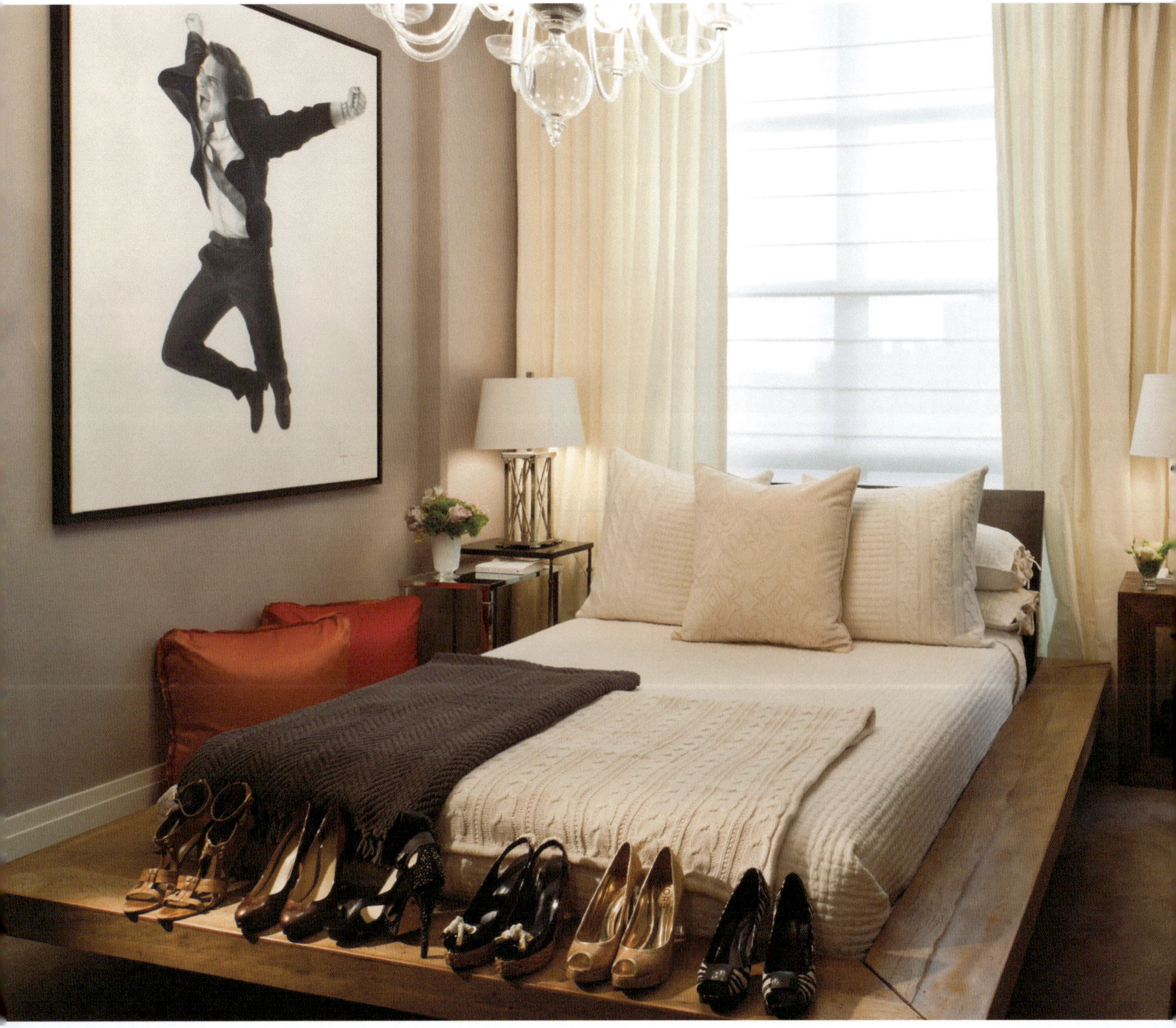

A beautiful feminine room. Elizabeth Cb Marsh, who designed this room, craftily takes the typical sweetness out of the pink by graying it down very slightly. She then adds strong masculine elements, such as the black in the large picture or the geometry in the lamps, and creates a sparkling look. She gives this very small room a much larger impression and luxuriant quality without overwhelming such a confined space.

A beautiful soft, earthy pink can be found in stones and marble. These light gray shades of pink are beautiful for creating a serene atmosphere.

A pink that has been toned down with a slight mixture of black, creating almost a neutral beige, looks extremely elegant and meditative. It is very relaxing for a bedroom.

Rococo Pastels Add A Romantic Touch To The Small Bedroom

The preferred colors of the Rococo Period were a delicate powdered lilac, gray blue or rose combined with crème or white, and accents of gold. These hues can be beautifully interpreted into modern designs to add a poetic and gentle quality to a room. By using the light hues belonging to the family of blue or lilac, from almost gray, to powdered and pastel watercolor shades, you can create a shy but noble interaction of these subtle tones. Off-white or ivory will round up this color scheme. They are colors that express an inner privacy, a respect of values and have an extreme calming effect.

It is easy to ensure a lavish mood using lots of textiles and thick, fluffy carpets. The fabrics will add a subtle, luxurious note. Lace, wool and linen with tonal embroidery will create a warm mood and add an exclusive status to a modestly sized room. When concentrating on one, light shade, but playing with all its subtle nuances, it will be easy to create a light, playful mood. This will automatically occur when you work with different types of fabrics. Every fabric, wool or silk, reflects the color differently, so that this ensures a subtle variation of the same shade. Contrasting the textiles, brocade with linen, velvet with silk, also adds depth to the pastel room.

An off-white floor, white wooden furniture and accents of shiny metal conjures up a feminine, rococo style. You can create a masculine touch by using pure cotton, with a sporty look for the textiles, and adding furniture with a minimalistic, clear-cut style. The serenity and elegance remains, but the romantic, soft quality will diminish. Either way, the small bedroom will certainly have a charismatic quality of rococo charm.

The tendency to give a color a one-sided attribute can prevent it being used to its advantage. Even a delicate color can look very powerful depending on the task, on contrasts and on the environment. Naturally, it is an ideal color for the small bedroom. It has a natural relaxing quality about it. Combined with cream, it makes your heavy, tired muscles seem weightless and allows you to fall into a deep sense of relaxation.

Many men find pink too feminine. They have a problem sometimes of appearing too sensitive or sentimental. However, those who appreciate this hue are often extremely intuitive and subtle in their perception. Just as the subtle naturals in stones and in the barks of trees, pink has many refined hues in its color family, that can give a room softness but without appearing too feminine.

There are many shades of pink, depending it they are derived from red, magenta or purple. In addition, when they are grayed down with black, a whole new family of nuances come to life. Combine these with cream to create a gentle atmosphere.

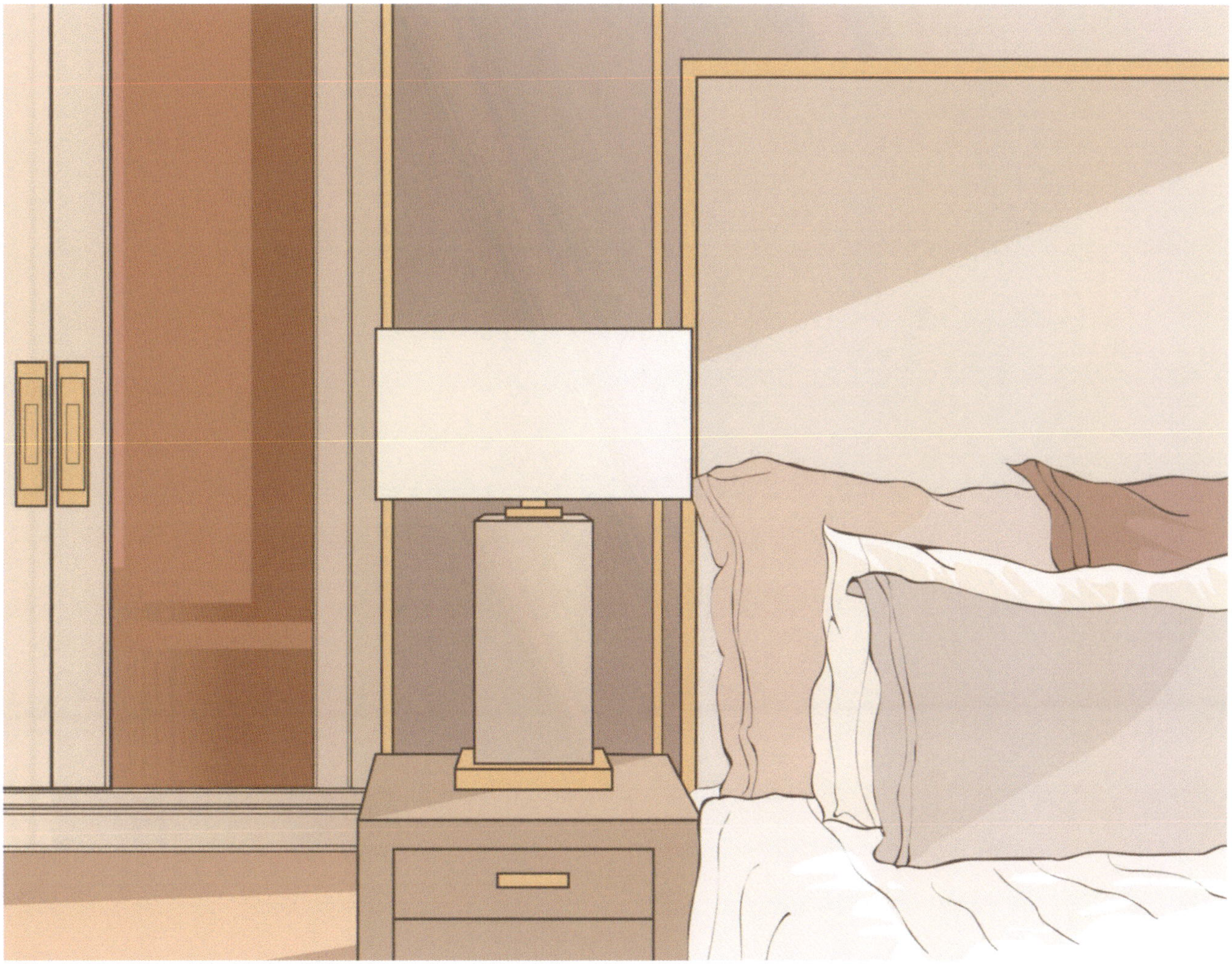

Powder blue combined with white, creams or naturals create that Rococo experience of lightness and transparency.

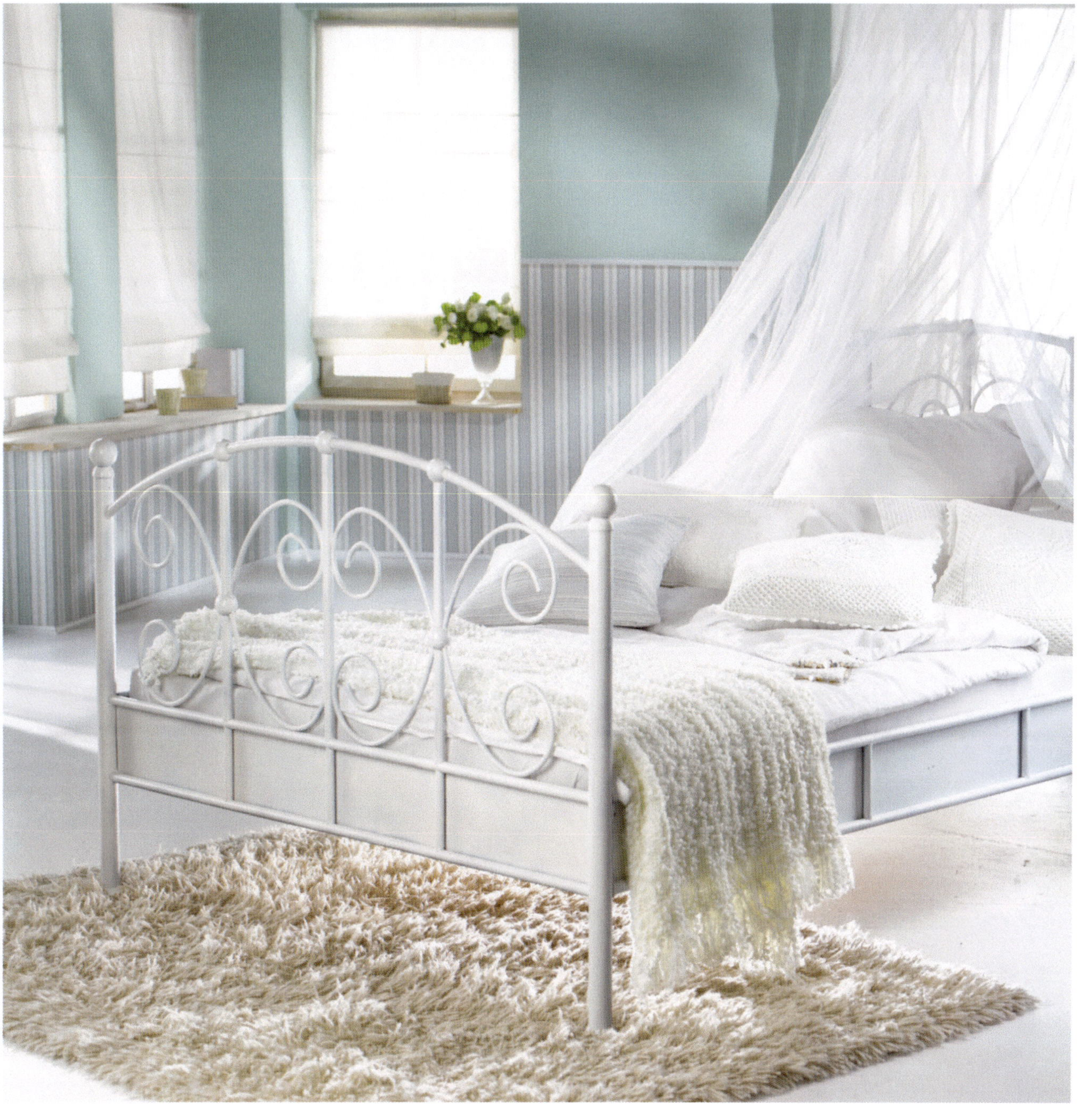

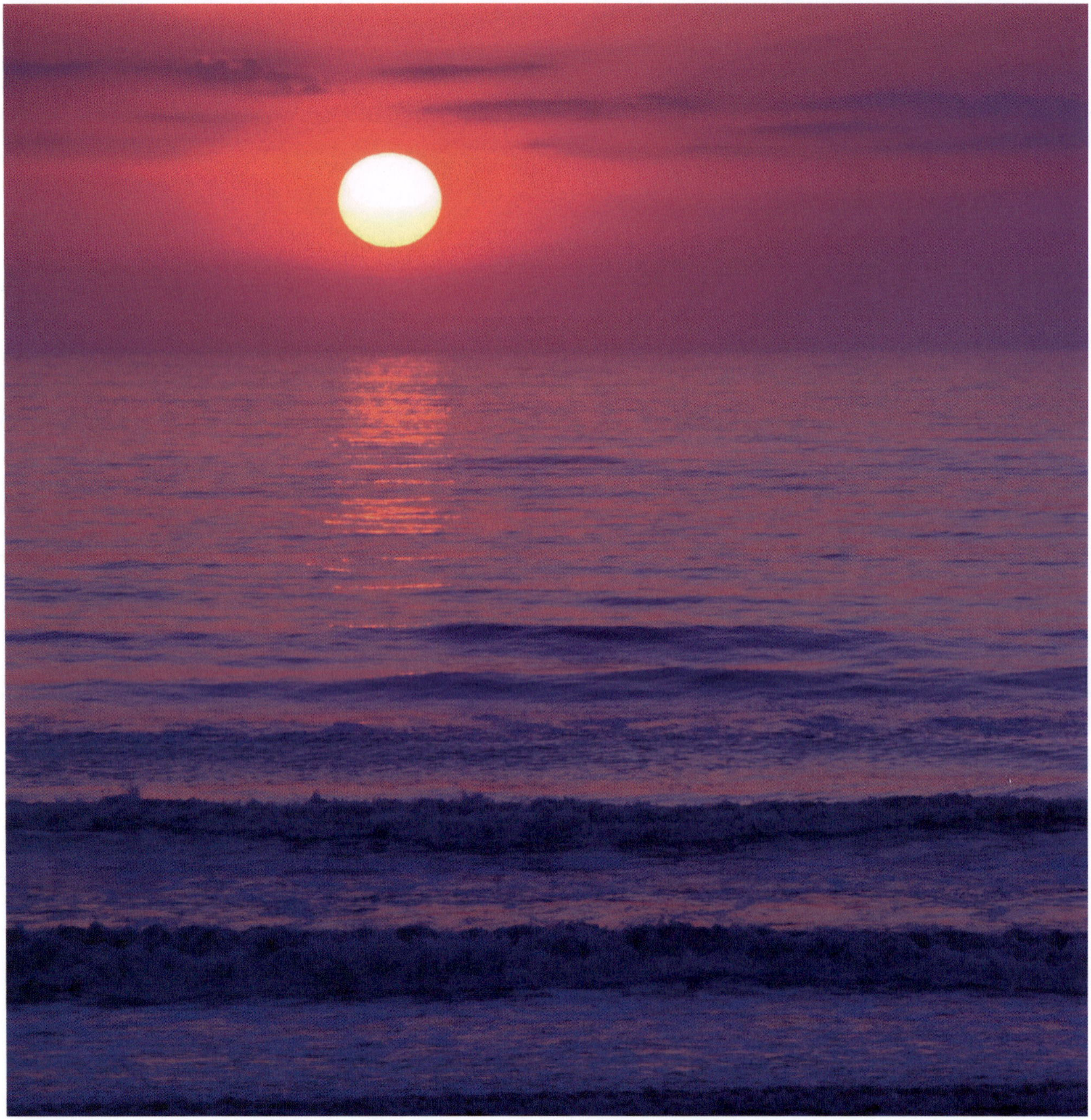

Violet Creates A Contemplative Mood

Violet is associated with religion and meditation. If can look very distinctive when used carefully for living areas. It will certainly add a dignified and elite quality to a room. The lighter shades of violet and the light pink shades of purple are excellent for creating a charming quality in a bedroom. There are so many shades and when used in various patterns it is easy to mix and match stripes and florals. This will create a friendly atmosphere which will still be peaceful and relaxing.

It takes a good hand to combine the pale shades of rose, lilac and mauve to avoid them looking insipid. They gain depth when combined with a sandalwood brown or stone gray. When cleverly combined, these delicate pastels have a special, poetic beauty. They look exquisite when used for flowing materials, such as shimmering silks, satins, soft wools, and fine cotton. Since these hues cannot be clearly defined, they change continually according to the light, which gives them added subtleness.

Furniture made of metal, or with very clear lines, will also add to the refinement and create a dignified contrast to these delicate hues. The grayish tones of pink and lavender, in combination with grays, browns and crème, will give the small room an extremely beautiful touch of luxury. These pastel hues will also make the small room seem much larger. The interplay of various materials, such as wool and silk, iron and wood, cotton and stone, will add a subtle interaction of contrasts, giving the small room a rich sense of understatement.

Purple has various shades from a warm bright purple to a more meditative bluish hue.

A bluish purple is combined with its complementary, a warm yellow, in the carpet and wood. White accents emphasize a sense of purity.

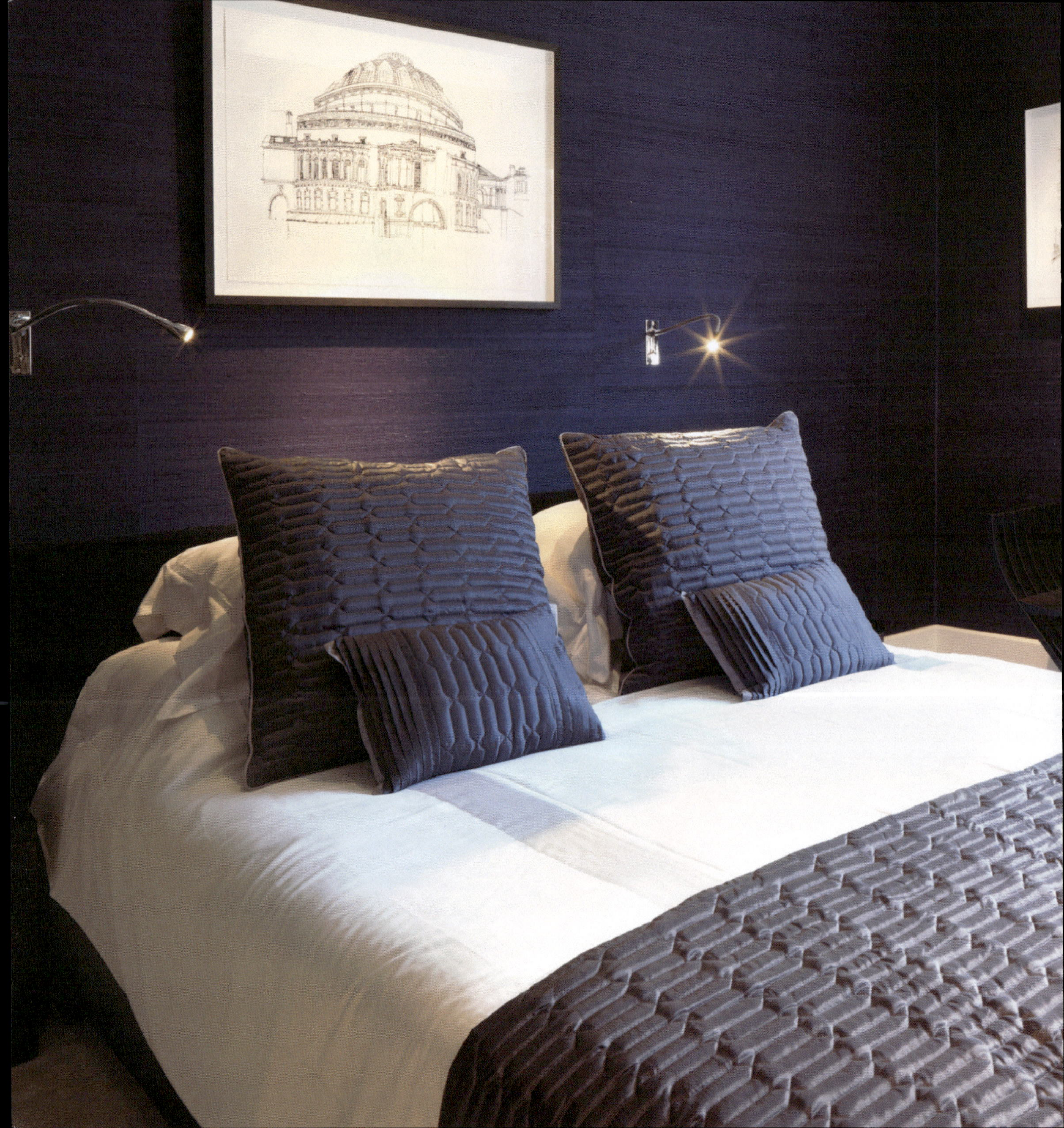

A lovely calm guest room designed by Tracy Leach @ Icon Interiors: A cool dark purple, almost indigo blue, gives the impression of a bright moonlight night. This quality is enhanced by the small star like lamps and the decorative pictures that are in bright contrast to the dark color of the walls.

Purple is ideal for creating a wellness atmosphere.

Purple has beautiful light shades that when slightly grayed down create extremely elegant hues for the walls. When accents of the primal purple color are added in curtains or accessories, they harmonize exquisitely with the more natural shades derived from its family of hues. Combine these with pure white for an exquisite atmosphere.

Green For A Peaceful Refuge

Green can transform the small bedroom into a beautiful refuge of peace, or make it charmingly innovative and alert. It is one of the most refreshing colors. It has such a tremendous variety of shades that the possibilities for creating individual and attractive small bedroom are considerable.

Since green is a very passive color, you can add a little more zest to the decor by using a mix and match of patterns within that one color. Or you can play with light and dark contrasts. Mixing large patterns with small ones, checks, stripes and poker dots, will all never seem overwhelming since green always remains as a center of calmness.

Green has its brighter shades too. A fully saturated green for accessories, contrasted with fresh white walls can look very abstract. This makes it ideal for those who love this color but like an ultra modern interior. Light spring green added sporadically to a room painted in cream white can look as light and jolly as a fresh spring day.

If you decide on green for the walls, it would be advisable to use a very light shade in combination with lots of white. This will ensure that the room does not appear even smaller than it actually is. If your bedroom happens to be long and narrow, you could paint a stronger shade of green on one of the walls at the far end of the room. This will make that particular wall project forward and improve the shape of the room, giving the impression that it is more rectangular.

Green and white can be repeated throughout the decor, for pictures, lamps and carpets. It naturally invites a theme of nature for accessories. This does not mean that the look must be traditional. On the contrary, you can find brilliant designs inspired by nature, but with extremely original and modern artistic interpretations.It is so easy to create a high impact and extremely attractive small bedroom, concentrating on one color. A chromatic color scheme is also easy to deal with if you are not very adept at mixing colors. Green is naturally one of the easiest colors to apply because of its peaceful nature.

138

Green inspires to eat healthy food for breakfast

|139

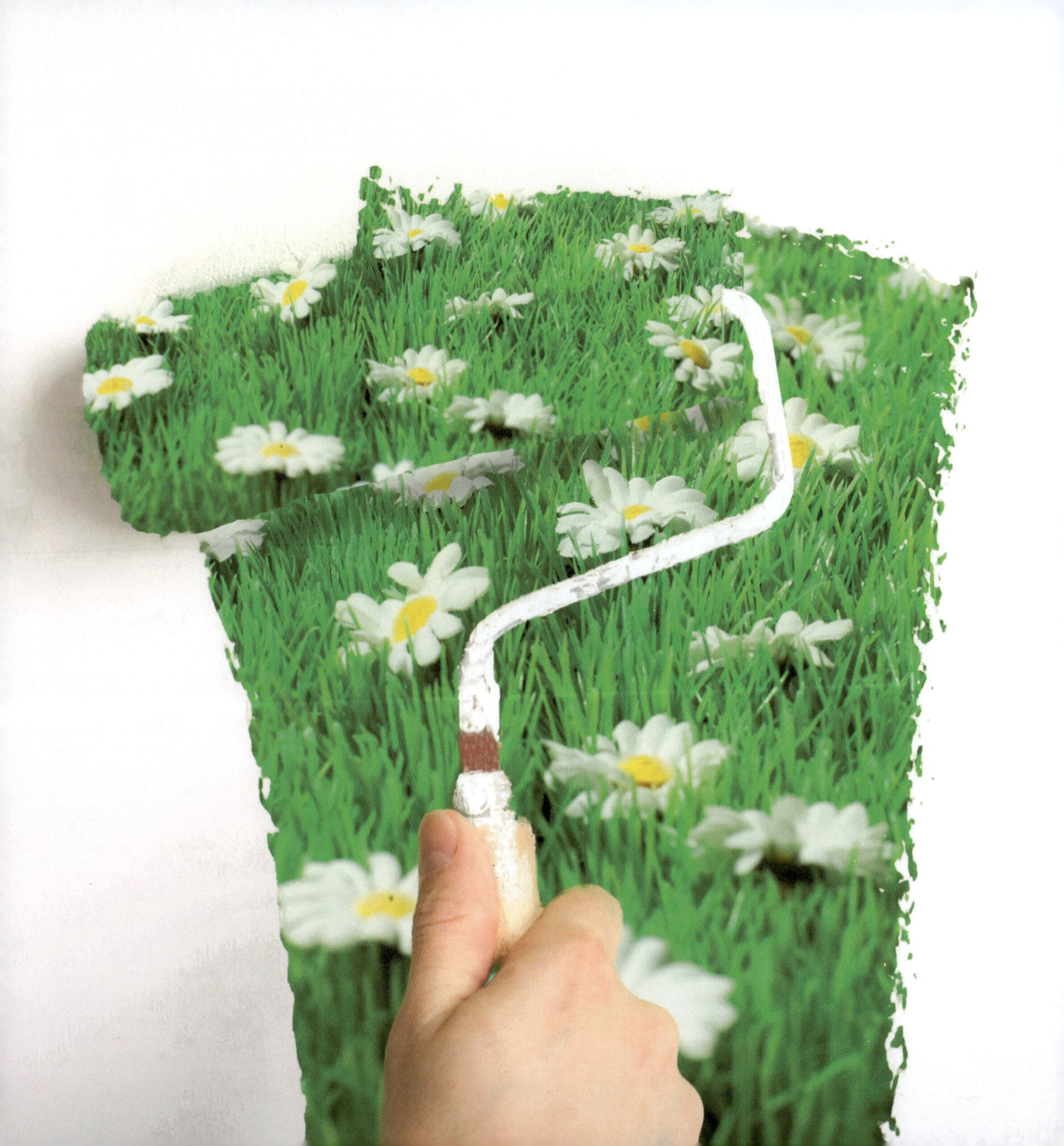

When you combine an emerald green or a pure grass green with white, you will achieve a highly brisk tenor that we rarely associate with this hue. It gives a small room the energy we experience during springtime when everything seems so fresh and vital.

Turquoise Serenity

Turquoise is a very calm and cool color. It is one of the coldest colors, even colder than a sky blue. As the color of ice and water, turquoise seems to conceal a subtle tension. Just as ice and water hide a completely different form of life from our view – the vegetation and diverse creatures of water – it almost seems that turquoise, when examined more closely, is concealing something mysterious. It is distant, elegant, and somewhat evasive. In comparison, the pale blue of the sky appears to be quite naive.

Turquoise is really in its element when used for the bathroom. Like ice and water, it can look very fresh and brisk. This color is often used in advertising for cosmetics and wellness products, as it symbolizes purity and youthfulness. Combined with white, it can add a touch of freshness to a small, dark bathroom and create a light, rejuvenating atmosphere.

Cool shades of turquoise are also charming to use for a small bedroom. It needs graying down a little to appease its cool aloofness. It can also make a very small room appear much larger. Since turquoise tends to make a space feel chilly, it can also lead to an increase in the costs for heating during the winter. It gives the impression that the room is colder than it actually is.

During winter, adding warm colors could counteract this problem. Towels, rugs and other accessories can be kept in a warm bright red or a bold, exhilarating orange. This way, the cool, elegant quality of turquoise will no longer be predominant. The warm colors will set the tone and create a warmer ambiance.

Warm sandy hues derived from orange or orange red are a natural complement to turquoise. If your bedroom looks too chilly, especially in winter, add some orange or orange red. Dark reddish wood also looks great in combination with turquoise.

145

Turquoise is excellent for a small bathroom. Combined with white it enlarges the bathroom and creates a calm and refreshing space.

You only need to add warm coral or orange hues and warm wood to take the chill out of the cool turquoise.

|147

A Rich Chocolate Brown For A Calming Ambiance

Since it has become known that dark chocolate is good for health and calming for the nerves, it has caused a revival of chocolate products with small chocolate stores appearing everywhere. The color of the chocolate, and all of the well-designed packaging for this appetizing product, evoke in themselves a sense of well-being. All shades of brown, as a basis for a color scheme for a bedroom, are not only extremely dignified, but also very relaxing.

A small bedroom decorated in brown can be turned into a perfect refuge, where life slows down a little. It will be a place where you can get in touch with the inner-self again. This hue, including its various shades, conveys a presence and a deep sense of tranquility. It is the color of earth and indeed brings us back to our roots.

Dark brown will make the tiny bedroom look even smaller. However, it conveys a sense of intimacy, of being protected and cared for. The different shades of brown, from a deep chocolate brown to a light coffee color, when contrasted with white and beige, provide depth and structure.

With blinders made of the diverse types of woven bast, you can add a Japanese elegance to a small room. Panels made of these fabrics would also look very sophisticated. They allow you to draw the panels back and forth, according to the amount of light you require. This would give the room a very purist, Japanese look.

Alternatively, you can create a sheer, medieval, textural richness by adding dark brown curtains made of shimmering brocades, smooth velvets, warm flannel or heavy, hand-woven linen. By making a bed-cover in the same material, you will create a totally unified look. The walls could be painted in a smooth coffee brown. Accessories in leather, dark wood and bronze would round up the luxurious effect.

Brown is so versatile, and there are many ways of adding an exquisite atmosphere to a small bedroom when using it as the basis for a color scheme. The end result will always be dignified and sophisticated, because of the very nature of this hue.

Brown is the color of so many natural textures. By combining the various textures and shades of brown you will breathe life into this subdued color without loosing its calmness.

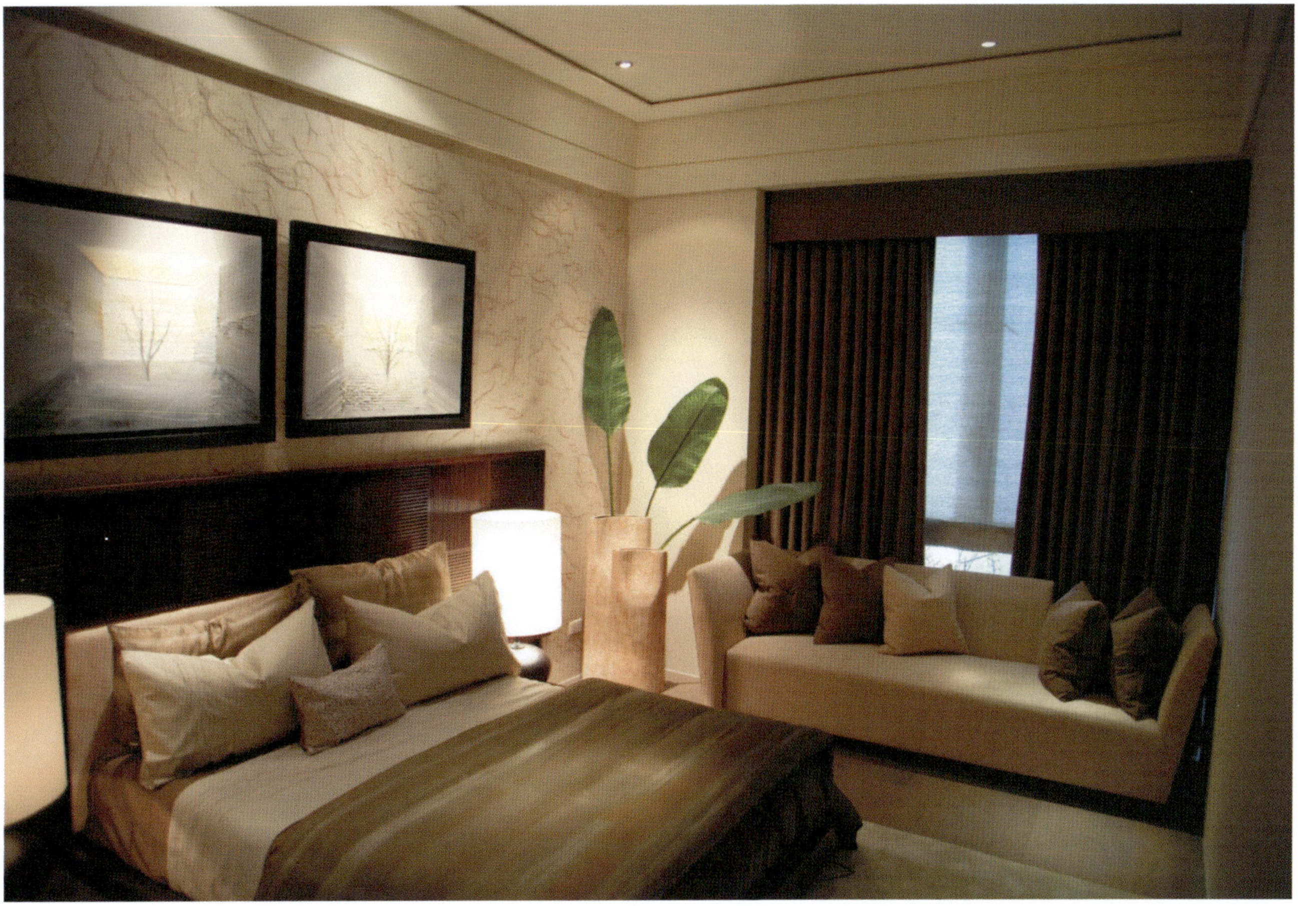

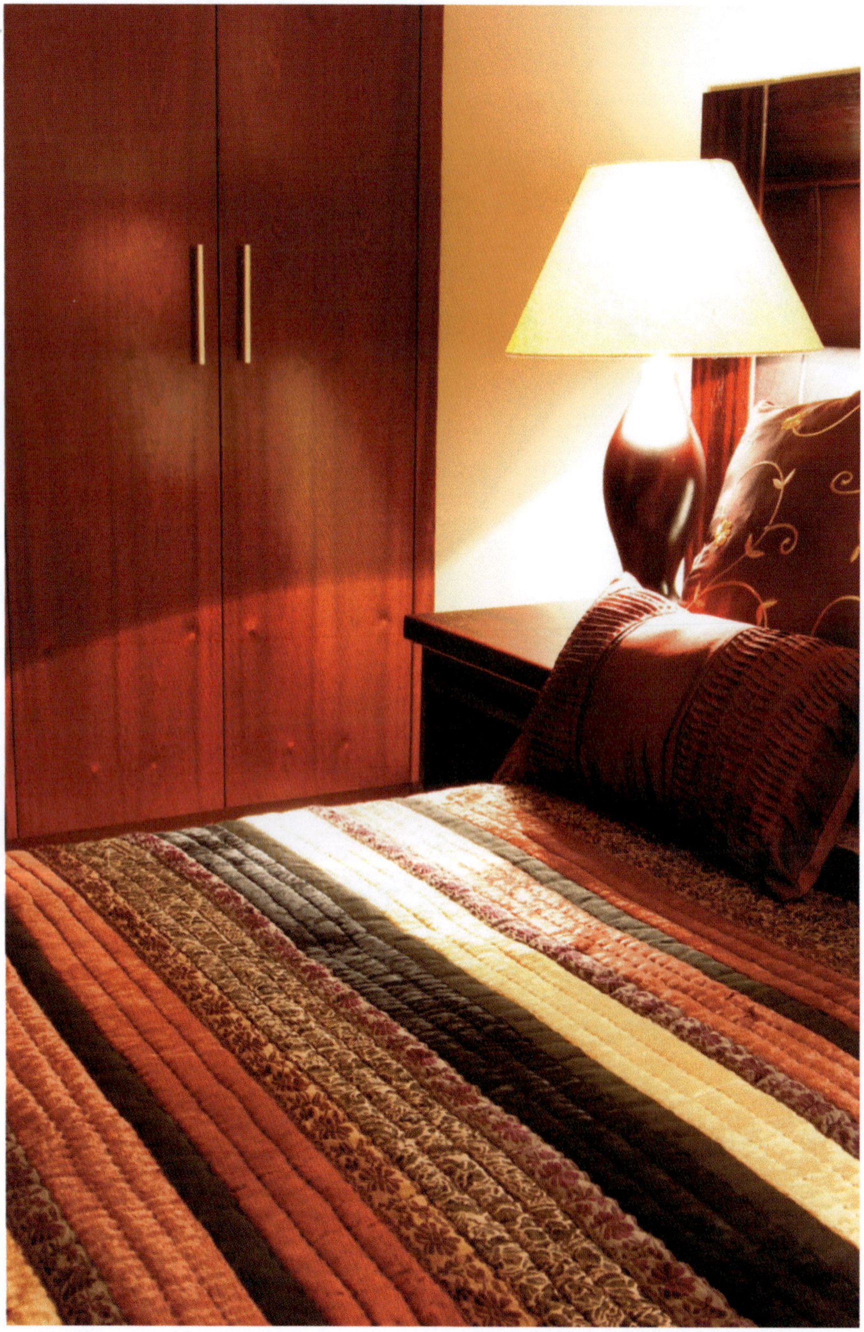

Assorted herbs and spices in warm terracotta and brown act as a gorgeous color scheme for a bedroom.

The interior designer, Marie Burgos, has converted this very narrow area into a spacious, serene, Zen-like bedroom. The warm chocolate color combined with neutrals and the Japanese inspired sliding doors give it a dignified, rich appearance.

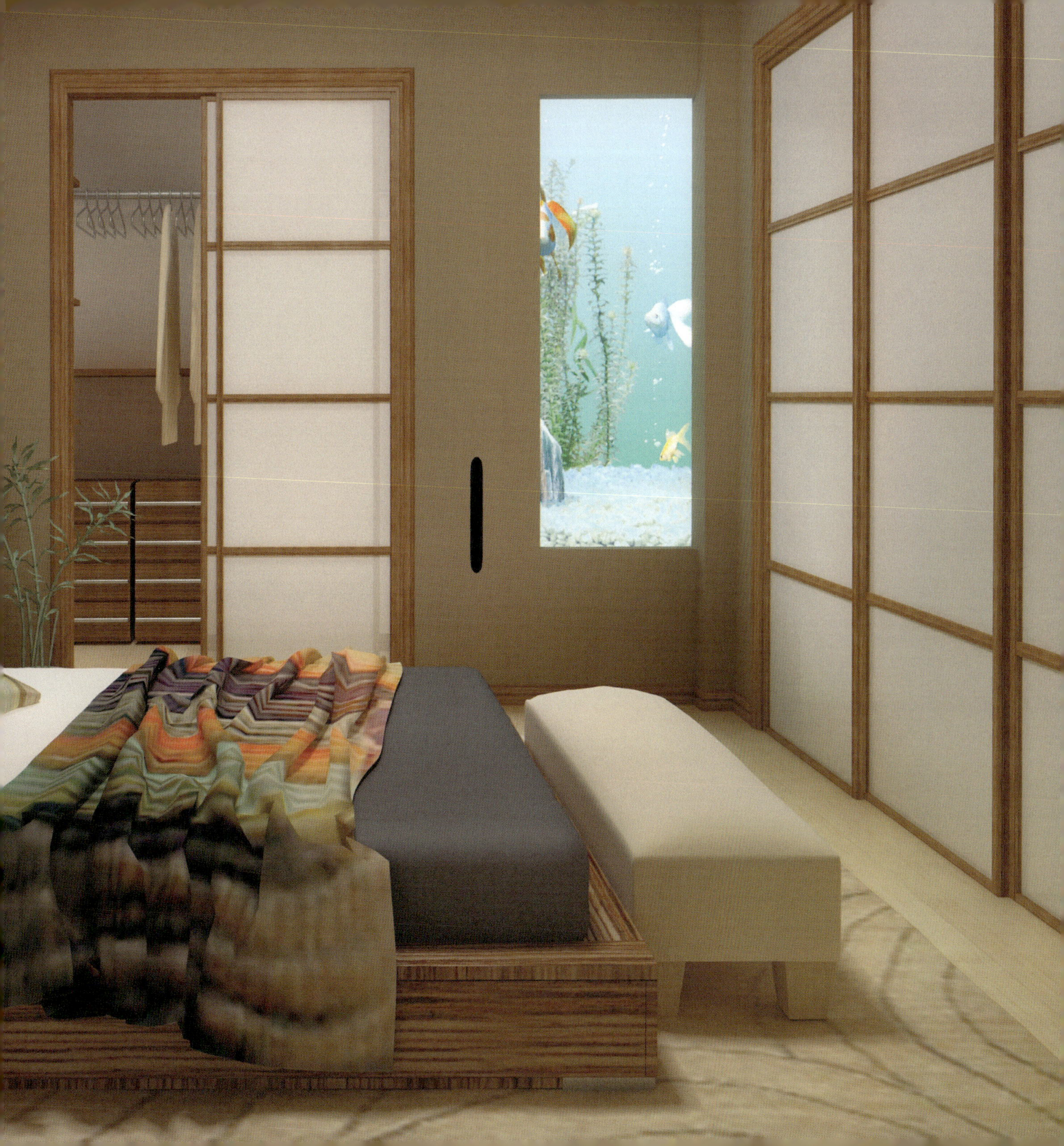

A restful light and brass fittings are ideal for a room that is designed with a warm brown as its color scheme.

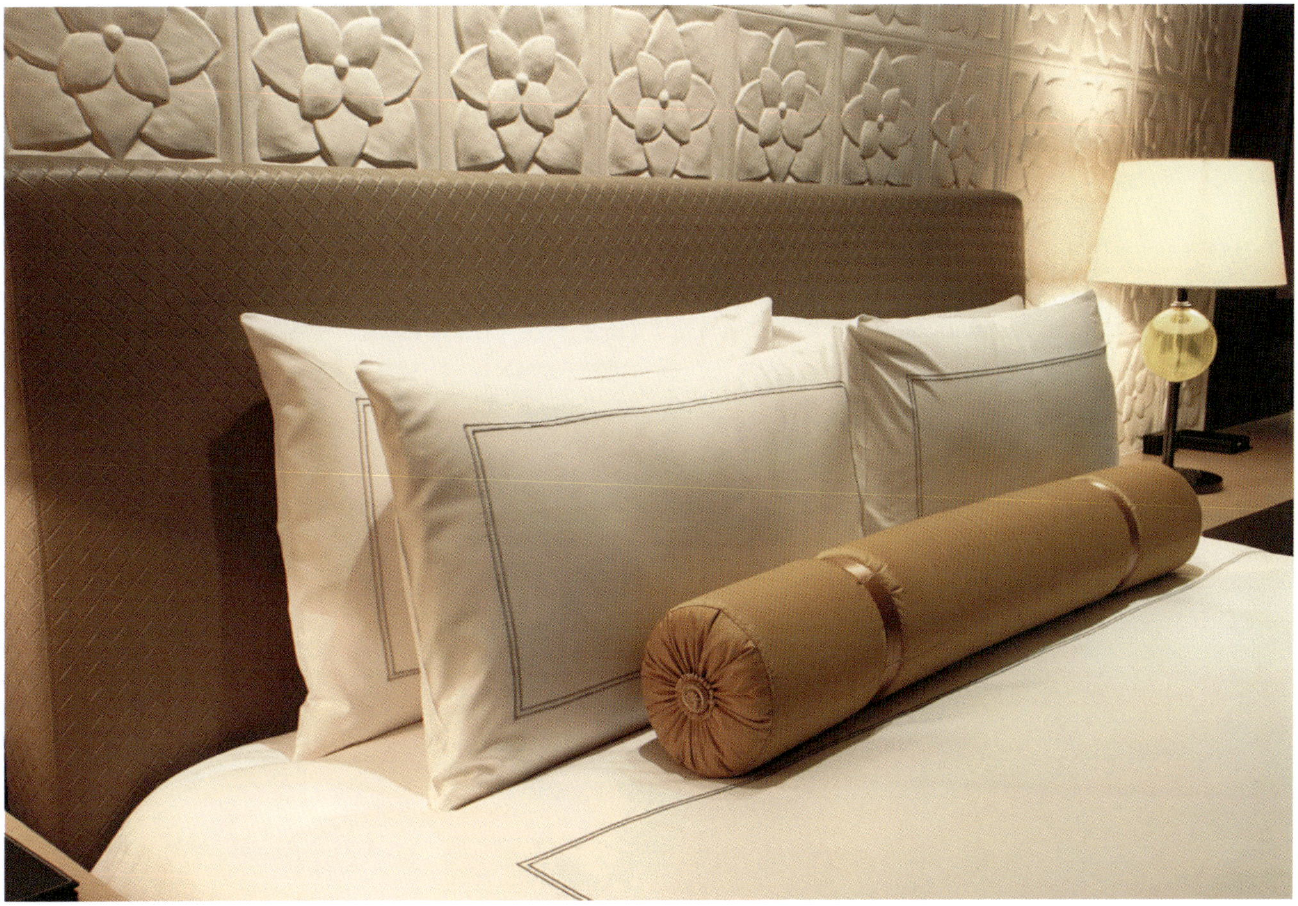

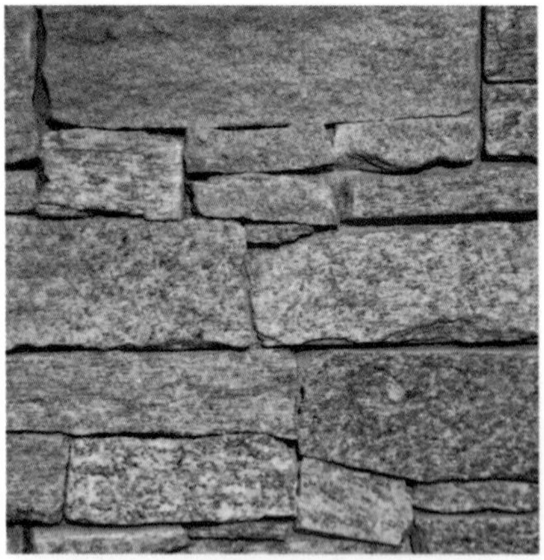
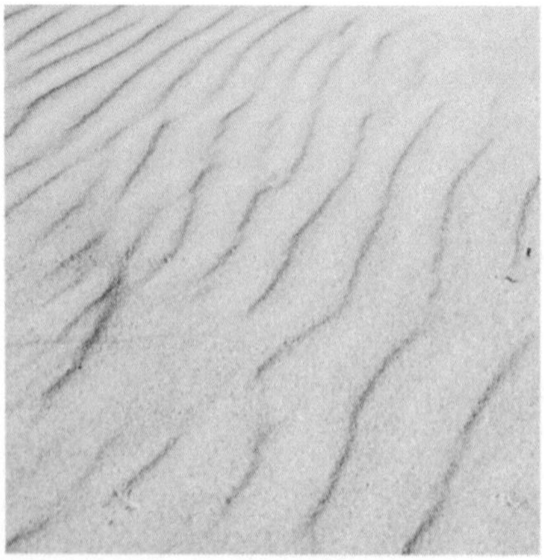
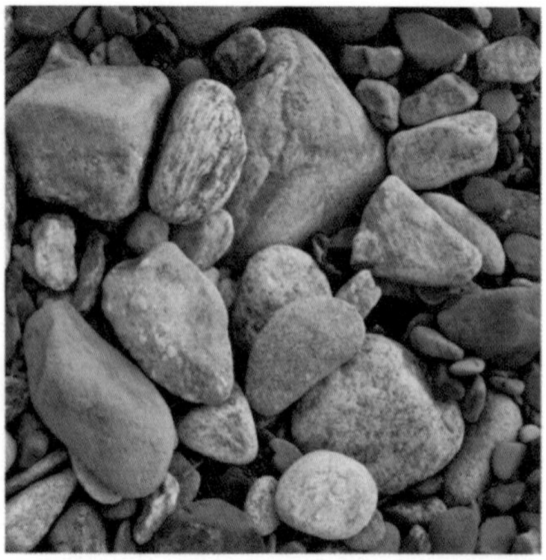
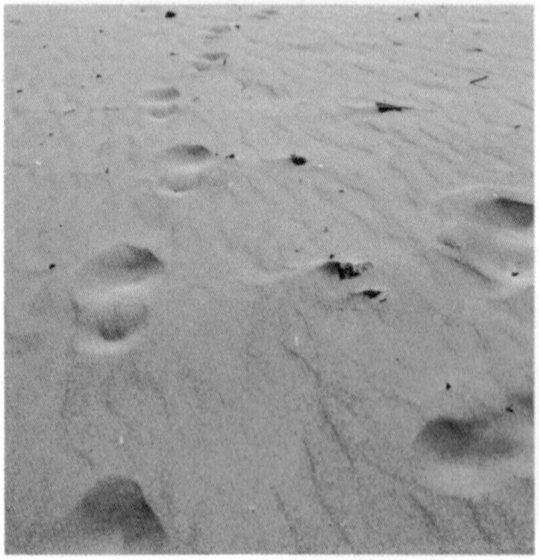
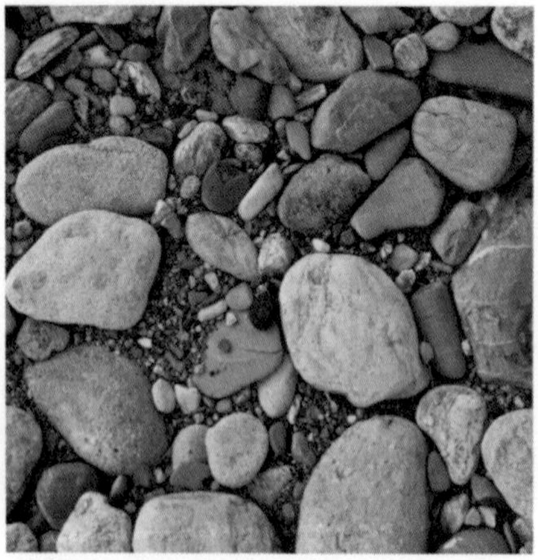
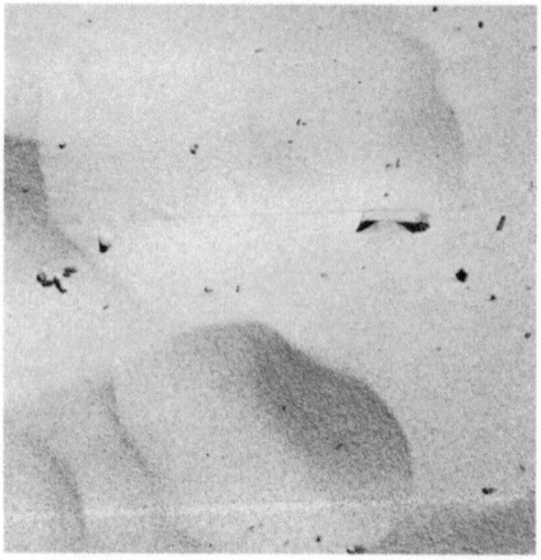
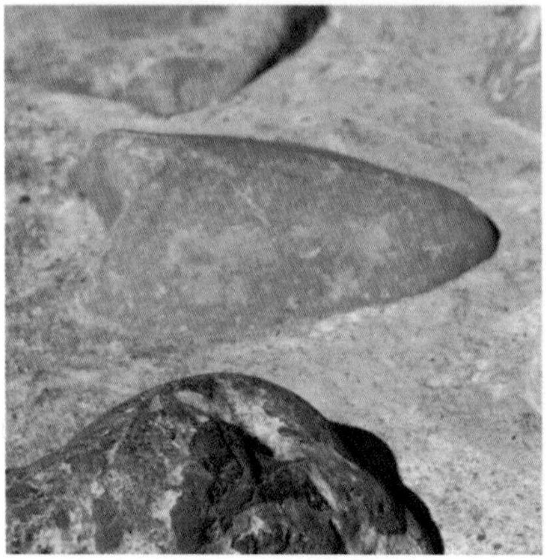
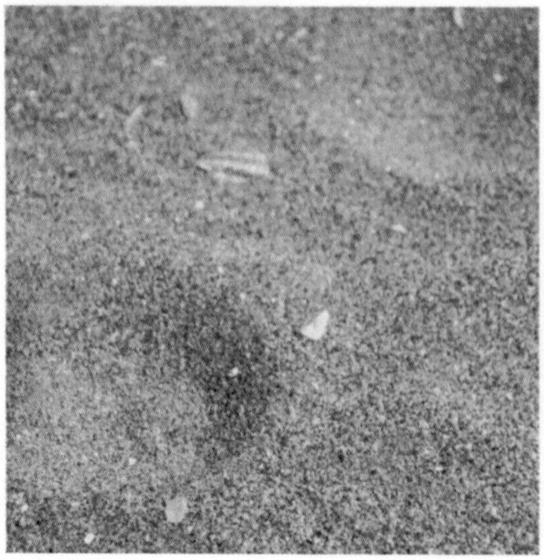
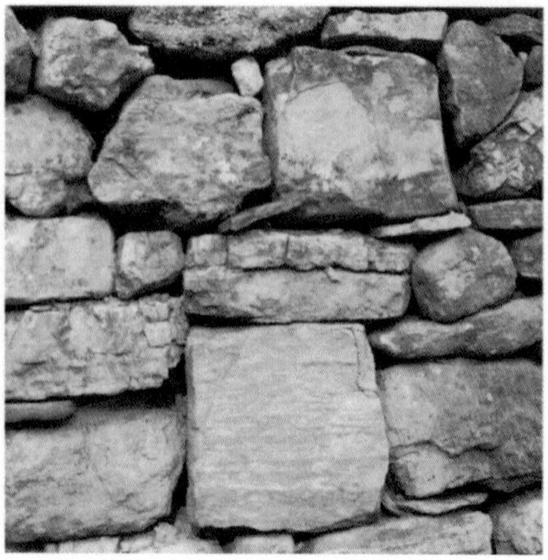

Naturals Add A Subtle Distinction To Small Spaces

Naturals never cease being fashionable. They have their roots in the structures that are surrounding us in nature; in stones that from a distance appear colorless only to reveal, as we get closer, such rich shades of crème, dove blues or grayed pinks. Subtle violet tinted beiges of the barks of trees or silky, fawn tones of a sandy beach and many other subtle tones can be discovered in these structures. They are a great source for natural hues.

Because the natural hues are deeply rooted in nature, they need not look rustic in color schemes for a bedroom. On the contrary, the neutral hues are great for emphasizing textural designs. The austere, high-tech look of some ultra-modern textiles can look extremely charming when combined with basket weaving and roughly structured linen. The interplay of natural hues unite the contrasting elements.

In fact, natural hues are great to emphasize surface effects: technical materials, such as plastic or metal, look great with structured wood, leather, hand-woven linen and fluffy rugs. By focusing on the essentials in furniture and decoration, and concentrating on the interplay of structures, a purist, even futuristic, or somewhat playful look can be created. A tiny bedroom can be transformed into a small and refined world of subtle contrasts that reflect the calming effect of timeless structure, making it a great place to find relaxation and a peace of mind.

Naturals are so easy to combine and always create a calming quality. By using lots of contrasting structures, such as wood, linen, silk, cotton, wool and cashmere, the room will gain diversity.

|161

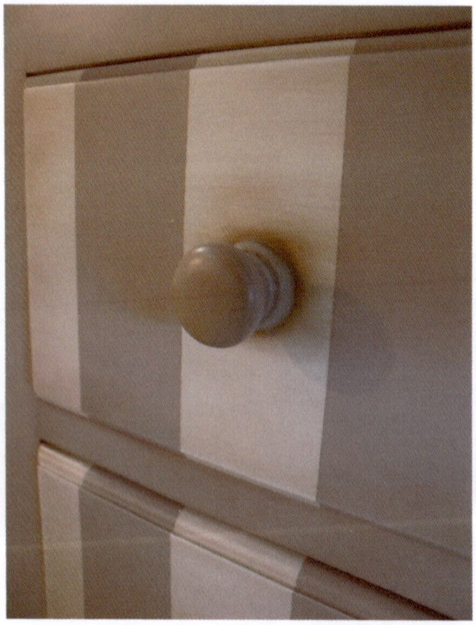

Even a children´s room can be effectively decorated with naturals. The various patterns animate their room and still leave lots of possibilities for adding their own works of art.

164

There are many toys for children available in all natural hues and materials that add even more charm to a small child´s bedroom based on beige and cream: And will not be overwhelmed by bright colorful accents.

Colors And Styles For The Windows

In small spaces, the windows play a very important part in the total color scheme. According to how they are decorated, they can in fact almost look like a piece of art work. Sometimes the window is the only way to create a decorative accent to the room.

If you are looking to create a spacious effect, panels are ideal. They hardly take up any space whatsoever and you can have them made in any type of material. When carefully chosen to match the total color scheme, they can emphasize a special theme, or can even be a major artistic center piece.

If you want to create a more romantic or cozy atmosphere, naturally curtains made of beautiful materials are ideal. They will add more intimacy to the room. Since they require more space, it is important to match the hues up well with the various shades used for the wall decoration and for bed covers. Alternatively, you can use light-weighted material.

|167

Soft flowing materials that are extremely finely woven and take up little space are ideal for the small bedroom and are available in almost every hue.

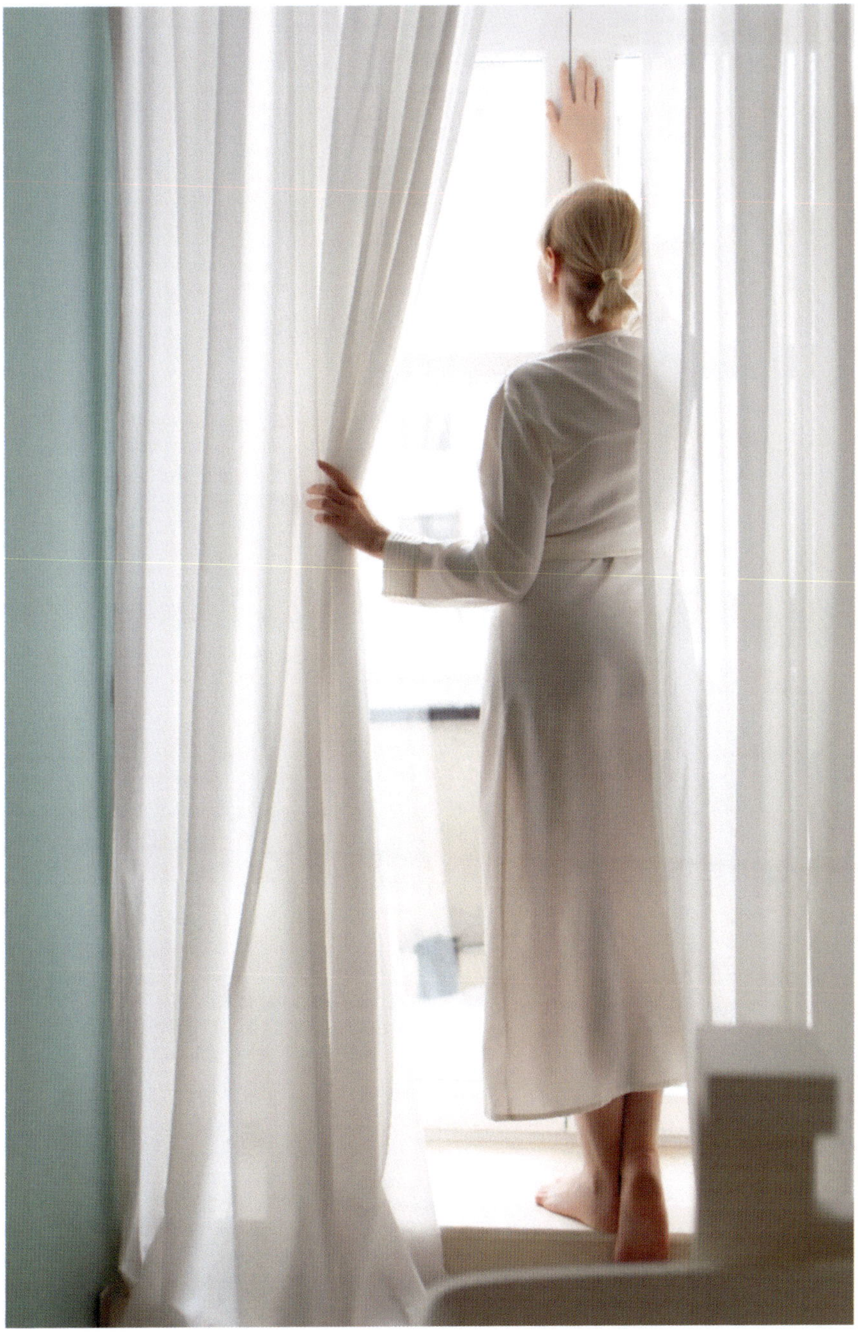

Patterns in curtains can help to bring a color scheme together, such as blue and naturals.

You can use the curtains to add a dramatic accent to the room .

|171

Panels for the window are ideal since they take up so little space and look very elegant.

Rollos fit so well into window spaces

Venetian Blinds

These evergreens never seem to go out of fashion. For those who love light they are ideal since they let the sunlight filter beautifully into the room. Since they can be perfectly fitted into the windows, they take up no space and they create a neat, uncluttered effect. This is ideal for small rooms. Particularly rooms kept in a minimalistic design will profit from their neat appearance.

Plissee Shades

More elegant than venetian blinds, plissee shades create a very gentle, dispersed light, yet share the same clear design. Plissee shades are an excellent solution for a room that has very little space. They are available in almost every hue and can easily be adapted to the color scheme of a room.

Venetian blinds or plissee shades will give even difficult windows definition and make them part of the decorative elements in a small room.

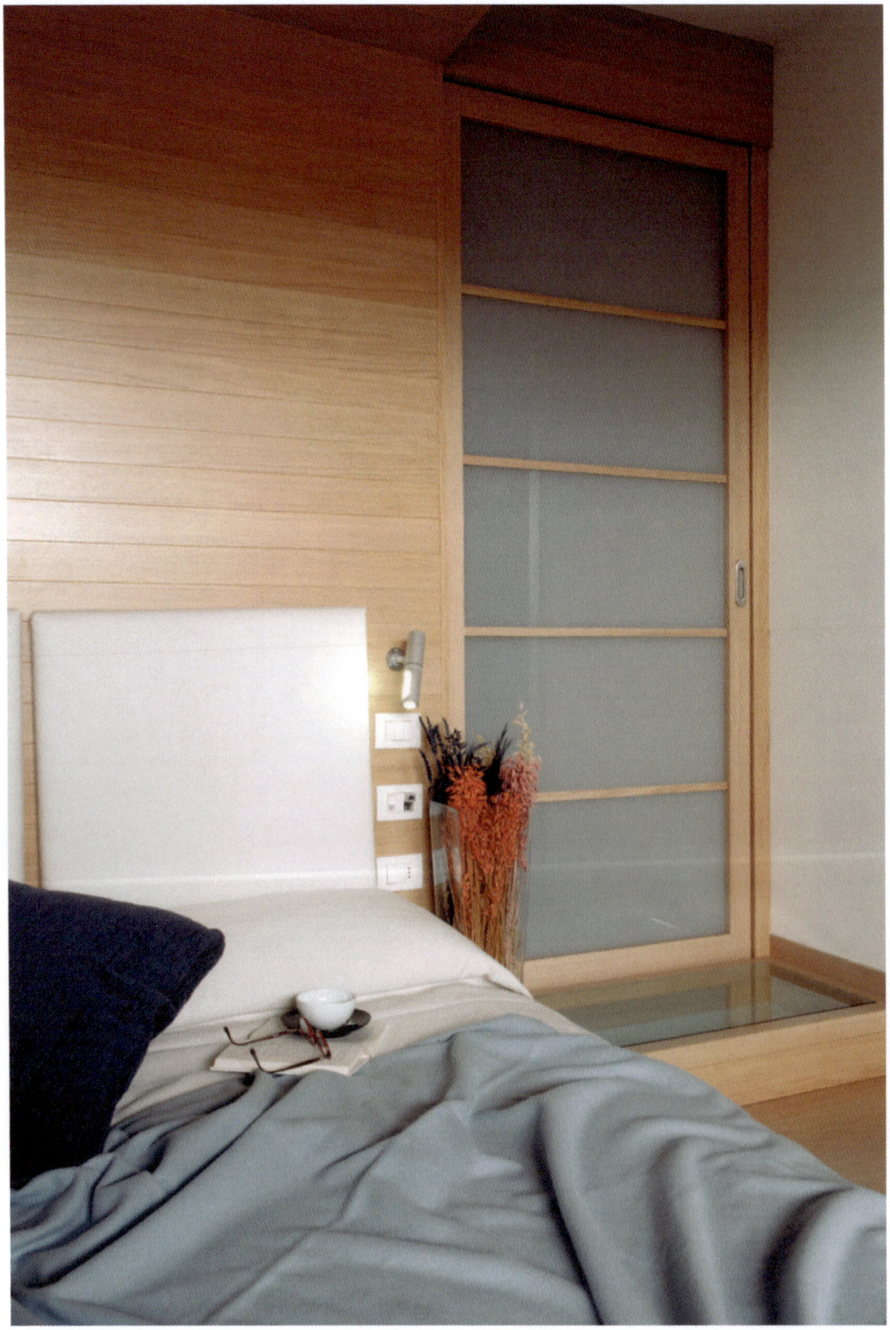

When a room is so small everything counts for creating a special ambiance. Sometimes small windows are the only possibility for giving the room a special quality. It is worth spending a little time in choosing the perfect window decoration. The smallest accents make such a big difference.

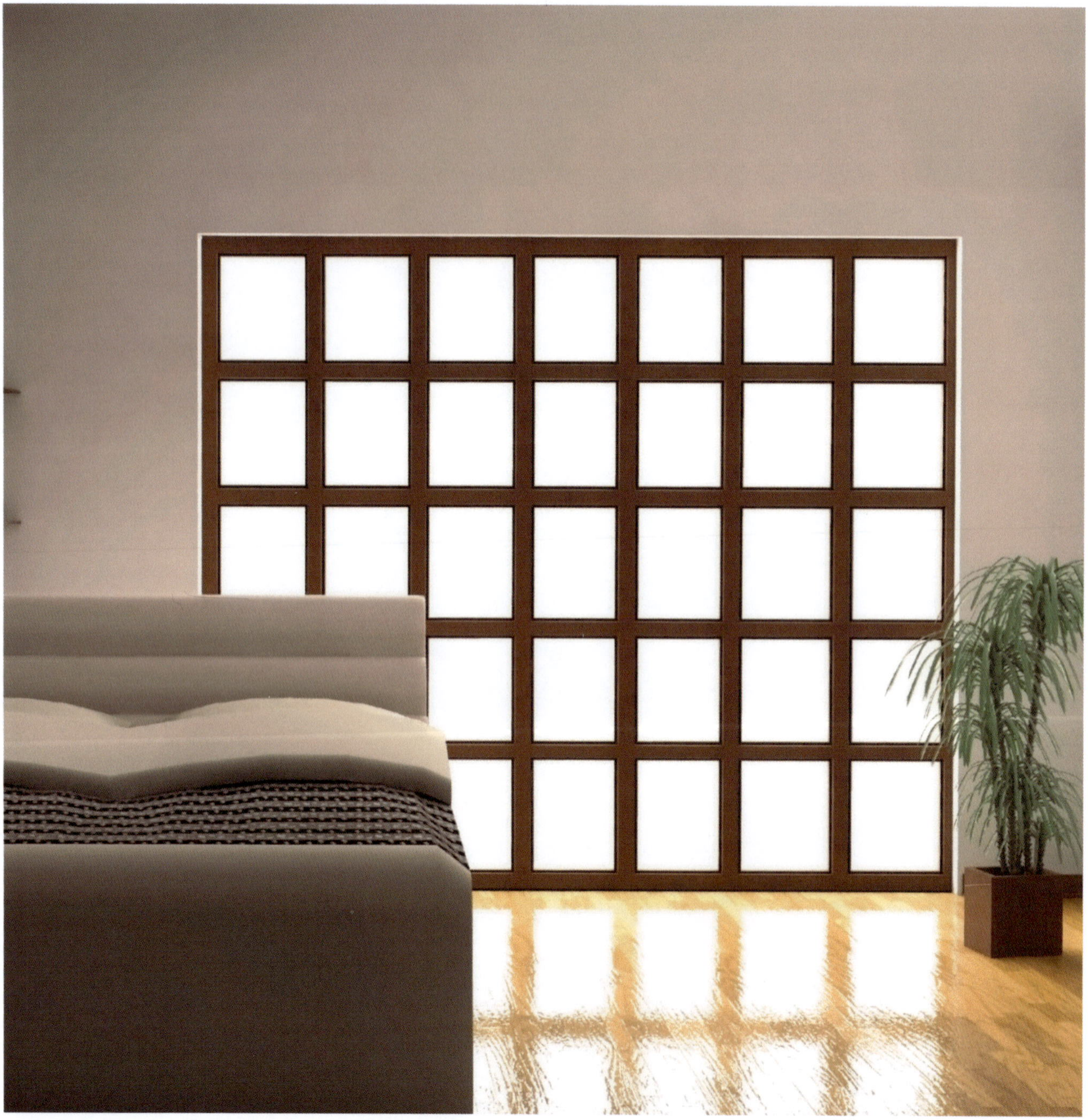

Lattice work for the windows is very expressive and at the same time serene.

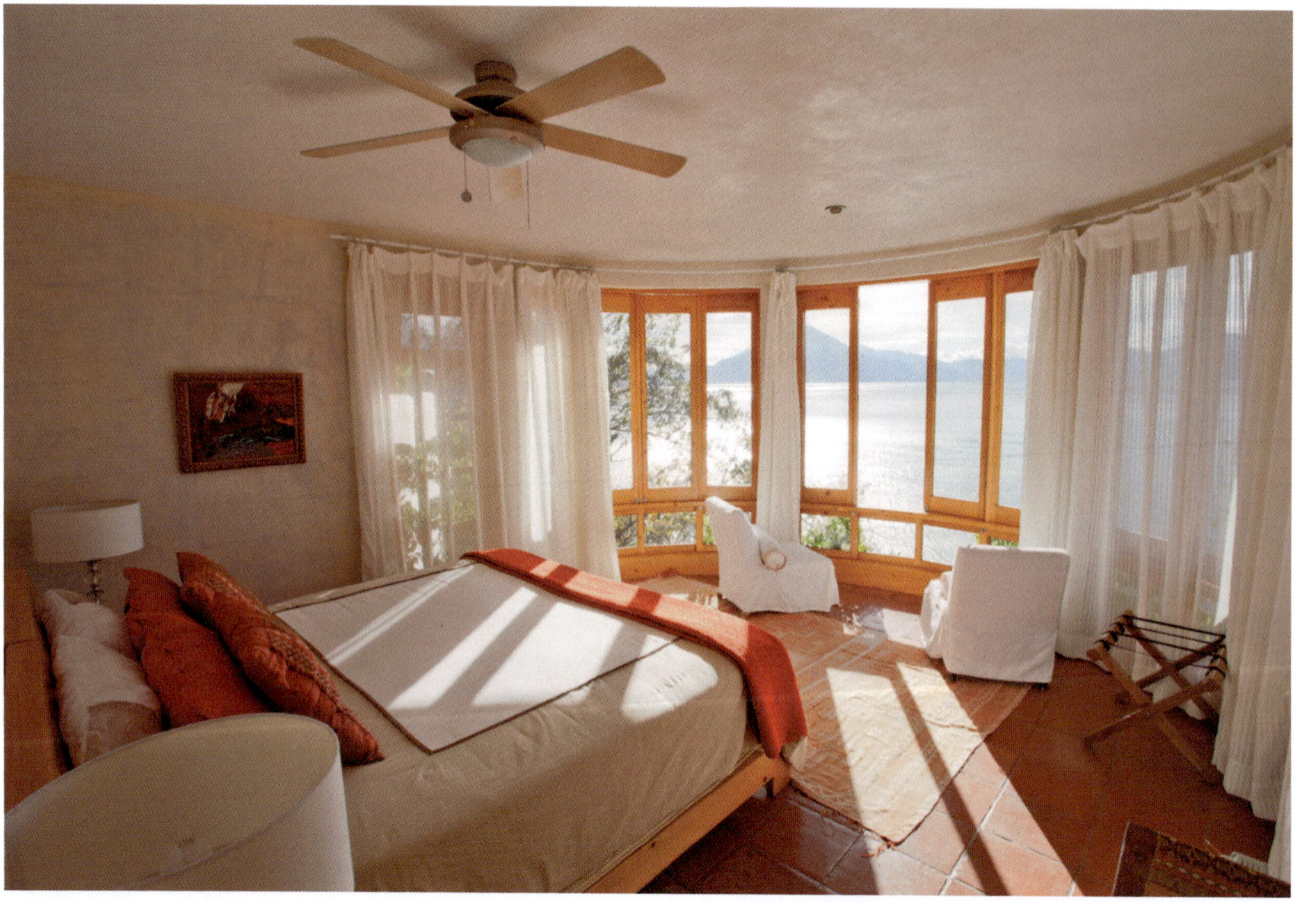

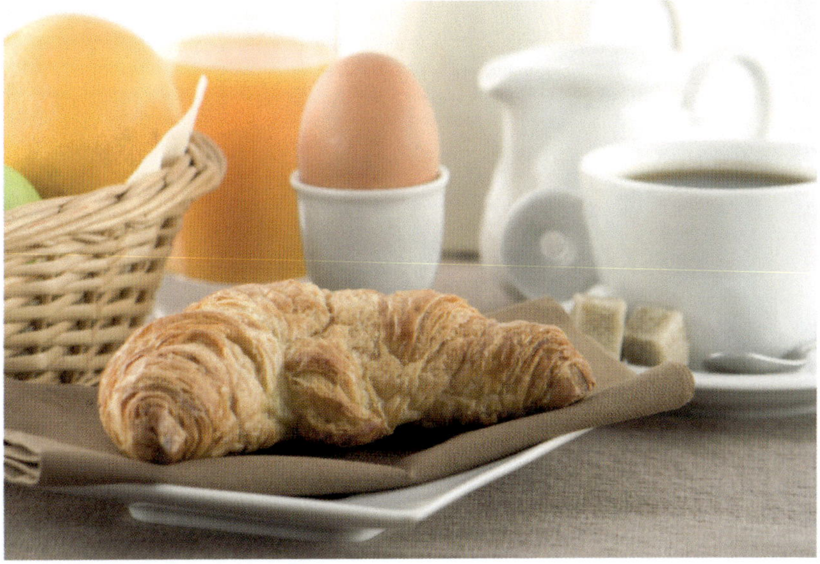

Bed Linen

Although you can design a room with little investment and still make it look luxurious and precious, it is advisable not to try to save on costs for bed linen.

We spend at least one third of our time in bed. Bed linen needs to be washed very often and poor quality will look shabby within a short period. Good quality is not only very pleasant for the touch, but is manufactured so that it will retain its beauty for many years even through the weekly laundry.

Good quality bed linen is made of superior cotton. It is woven to a high thread count which means it produces a soft silky feel to it that even improves with each and every wash.

It it always wise to buy a well-known brand. Such companies have been manufacturing bed linen in cotton and silk for many years and use a high degree of craftsmanship for the production of their products.

Bed linen has to be well sewn to endure the many years of wear and tear, as well as the friction that occurs in a washing machine. Good companies are committed to customer satisfaction which is a reason they are still in business.

|183

Often the bed linen also has an important decorative task and sometimes, especially in very small bedrooms, is the main focus of attention. Good brands are always investing in new ideas and are coming up with innovative ideas all the time.

When you decide on a color scheme for the bedroom, it becomes easy to build up a collection of bed linen over the years that will easily mix and match.

You can combine modern patterns with classical stripes, checks and structures; or contrast materials such as exquisitely detailed embroidery with raw linen. You can give the bed a touch of sheer luxury with shimmering satin.

Since you will be remaining within your chosen color scheme, you will find yourself creating your very own individual combinations that relate to each other perfectly, thanks to a distinct color statement.

Sometimes, just one large, expressive pattern can be varied by combining it with the various shades of color in the sheets.

|185

Interior Designer Credits

Kia Sunda | Pages 54 and 55

Kia is founder of Kia Designs. With over 10 years experience within the Interior Design Industry, she has gained a reputation for innovative design and has collected an array of awards, including being named as one of "The Top Ten Young Designers in the UK" by IDFX Magazine.

Contact Information:
Kia Sunda
www.kiadesigns.co.uk
123 Grosvenor Avenue,
London, Greater London,
United Kingdom, N5 2NL
Phone +44 7912138822

Kathryn Johnson | Pages 80 and 81

Kathryn Johnson is an experienced designer familiar with the design of a number of architectual styles. From cottage to post modern her beautiful homes and remodels have been featured in several magazines and newspapers.

Contact Information:
Kathryn Johnson Interiors Inc.
kathryn@kjinteriorsinc.com
4205 Minnesota Lane North
Plymouth, Mn. 55446
Phone 612 423 5014

Photography: Mark Ehlen - Ehlen Creative
www.ehlencreative.com

Charmean Neithart | Pages 90 and 91

Charmean Neithart is founder of Charmean Neithart Interiors, LLC. Charmean Neithart listens to your story and the journey that brought you to this point. She then creates an environment that serves as the backdrop of your daily life. Each story, and ultimately each home, possesses unique qualities. Charmean's desire is to find the thread that intertwines the story with the space and transform it into a functional living environment.

Contact Information:
www.charmean-neithart-interiors.com
Charmean Neithart Interiors, LLC.
Pasadena, CA, US 91106
Phone 626 441 4288

Photography: Erika Bierman
www.erikabiermanphotography.com

Neslihan Pekcan | Pages 94 and 95

Neslihan Pekcan studied Interior Design at the Savannah College of Art and Design "Interior Design Department" USA, before returning to her home country, Turkey. She founded her Pebbledesign company in Instanbul in 2004 and has since been focusing on designing for residential and commercial purposes as well as restaurants, cafes and yachts.

Contact Information:
www.pebble-design.com
Neslihan Pekcan of Pebble Design
Nispetiye cad. Belediye sitesi A3 Blok No:26 Etiler,
Istanbul, Turkey

Phone +90 212 3517790
Fax +90 212 3517723

Elizabeth Cb Marsh | Pages 118 and 119

Elizabeth Cb Marsh (formerly Cross-Beard) began her career over a decade ago in interior design and architecture at a Baltimore based architectural firm. Shortly after, she was recruited to join Jenkins Baer Associates as a high-end residential designer, and has been with the firm ever since. As an associate designer, she works with her clients to bring their visions to life - melding traditional and modern into a sophisticated palette that is as unique as each client and home.

Contact information:
www.jenkinsbaer.com
Elizabeth Cb Marsh

Associate Interior Designer
eliz@jenkinsbaer.com
Jenkins Baer Associates
24 W Chase Street
Baltimore, MD 21201
Phone 410 727 4100
Fax 410 727 4130

Photographer: Kafka Curtis Martin

Tracy Leach Pages | 132 and 133

Tracy Leach is the founder Icon Interiors Co in the UK. Her company offers Interior Design Services – specializing in residential properties and bespoke kitchens. In addition, she offers commercial interior design services for wedding venues and boutique hotels.

Contact Information
www.icon-interiors.co.uk
Tracy Leach
2 Greyhound Lane, Overton,
Basingstoke,
United Kingdom, RG25 3LE
Phone +44 0845 519 3441

Photographer: Steve Russel Studios

Marie Burgos | Pages 154 and 155

French native Marie Burgos founded her interior design firm in New York in 2007 with an emphasis on residential spaces which rapidly expended to commercial design. Marie's ultimate talent is understanding her client's needs and creating home, office and commercial interiors that are balanced, sophisticated, and highly functional. She also incorporates Feng Shui into her work.

Contact Information
Marie Burgos
www.marieburgosdesign.com
244 5th Avenue, Suite 288,
New York, New York,
United States, 10001
Phone 917 353 9149
Fax 212 726 3232

|189

Photography Credits

Title		Bedroom corner orange-yellow #40289755 © antonel - Fotolia.com
Page 2		Contemporary bedroom display. #19393083 © Barbara Helgason - Fotolia.com
Page 4		Hotel room with bed and wooden #40903436 ©witthaya - Fotolia.com
Page 5		Statue of Buddha #16802641 © Beboy - Fotolia.com
Page 6		Hotel room #24320978 #24320978 © Chefsamba - Fotolia.com
		Greece, gray and white room #41195998 © slava296 - Fotolia.com
Page 7		Blue bedroom interiore with navy bedding. #43562451 © Iriana Shiyan - Fotolia.com
		Modern red bedroom #42740565 © jacek_kadaj - Fotolia.com
Page 8		Anime bedroom #29839877 © nastazia - Fotolia.com
		Bedroom #20770486 © Monster - Fotolia.com
Page 9		Curtains in a room #41163468 © kanzefar - Fotolia.com
		Hotel room © iamnao #38575973 – Fotolia.com
Page 10		Bedroom corner orange-yellow #40289755 © antonel - Fotolia.com
Page 13		Contemporary Bedroom #36725464 © ep stock - Fotolia.com
Page 14		96 hues chromatic #26092317 © Unclesam - Fotolia.com
Page 16		Modern apartment interior #39833778 © Patryk Kosmider - Fotolia.com
Page 17		Color shades yellow and orange #30209184 © PAO joke - Fotolia.com
Page 18		Minimal romantic bedroom #29841150 © nastazia - Fotolia.com
Page 21		Red & white interior design plan © monamakela.com - Fotolia.com
Page 22		Painting brush with red #32914893 © krissi_21 - Fotolia.com
Page 25		Fashionable bedroom #37443743 © Mike Higginson - Fotolia.com
Page 26		Beautifully designed bedroom interior with shutters #6139820 © Paul Hill - Fotolia.com
Page 29		Kids bedroom with minimal modern design. #42832249 © Iriana Shiyan - Fotolia.com
Page 30		White flowers #43709557 © Maksim Shebeko - Fotolia.com
		A close-up of a white rose #39394604 © michaklootwijk - Fotolia.com
		Modern Design Vase	Architecture Interior #44029650 © XtravaganT - Fotolia.com
Page 31		A free flying white dove isolated #27062340 © Irochka - Fotolia.com
		Chandelier in white interior #2826536 © dzain - Fotolia.com
Page 32		Home Living #40789244 © brodtcast - Fotolia.com
Page 33		Hotel room #43737141 © topdeq - Fotolia.com
Page 35		Bed with a pillow and a cup of tea #42172012 © jannyjus - Fotolia.com
Page 36		Clock #10749942 © Friax74 - Fotolia.com
Page 37		Bedroom - Greece #41195998 © slava296 - Fotolia.com
Page 38		Strand an der Ostsee © tobitas #18343461 @Fotolia.com
Page 39		Amazing Bedroom with White Bed with Sea View © XtravaganT #44480381 - Fotolia.com
Page 40		Feather #23220548 © chairman - Fotolia.com
Page 42		Jewellry box #20684448 © Sergey Kohl - Fotolia.com
Page 43		A view of a modern bed room #9393463 © Ljupco Smokovski - Fotolia.com
Page 44		Beautiful Bedroom interior design #5862401 © Paul Hill – Fotolia.com
Page 45		Bedroom #36672966 © Grafvision - Fotolia.com
Page 46		Time Spiral #30887726 © rolffimages - Fotolia.com

Page 47	Postage stamp GB 1993 Marine Chronometer #36747350 © laufer - Fotolia.com
Page 49	Bedroom interior design. #42198076 © kosheen - Fotolia.com
Page 50	Bedroom #33794324 © alexandre zveiger - Fotolia.com
Page 51	Bengal cat stares outside #37528957 © steheap - Fotolia.com
Page 53	Hotel room #43737141 © topdeq - Fotolia.com
Pages 56 - 59	
	Ostsee #43053644 © PhotoSG - Fotolia.com
	Collage Ocean #18862980 © Stephanie Bandmann - Fotolia.com
	Water samples #15705884 © c - Fotolia.com
	Bedroom #22625828 © Nataliya Kashina - Fotolia.com
Page 58	Artistic minimal bedroom interior #29841197 © nastazia - Fotolia.com
Page 61	Extravagant Exclusive Design Bedroom with Ocean View #43309139 © XtravaganT - Fotolia.com
Page 62	Wardrobe #20773091 © KABUGUI - Fotolia.com
	Blueberries #43128607 © Sonja Birkelbach - Fotolia.com
	Retro lamp #22527399 © pixelfabrik - Fotolia.com
	Book #342196 © Franz Pfluegl - Fotolia.com
Page 63	Modern bedroom interior. © poligonchik #44120409 – Fotolia.com
Page 64	Laterne #38061234© Pixeltheater - Fotolia.com
Page 66	Sailing Boat Collage #33789960 © g-konzept.de - Fotolia.com
Page 67	Blue bedroom interiore with navy bedding. #43562451 © Iriana Shiyan - Fotolia.com
Page 68	Segelschiff 2 © danielschoenen #6235965 - Fotolia.com
Page 69	Bedroom © urbanlight #44624240
Page 71	Blue & white interior design planning #3312477 © monamakela.com - Fotolia.com
	Colorful pencils #44358846 © swisshippo - Fotolia.com
	Pattern #29558778 © inamai - Fotolia.com
	Seamless Blue Plaid Hearts Background Wallpaper #39005441 © songpixels - Fotolia.com
	Seamless pattern background with blue butterfly #42334502 © Terriana - Fotolia.com
	Checks_blue #14401855 © THesIMPLIFY - Fotolia.com
	Stripes - pattern 53876A #38680030 © guariscodmg - Fotolia.com
	Seamless pattern background with blue flowers #42007332 © Terriana - Fotolia.com
Page 72	Poppies field at sunset #32075750 © misu - Fotolia.com
Page 73	Hotel room #44009095 © graphistecs - Fotolia.com
Page 73	Red wine #27514254 © PhotoSG - Fotolia.com
Page 75	Bedding #25511872 © kim - Fotolia.com
Page 76	Modern red bedroom #42740565 © jacek_kadaj - Fotolia.com
Page 77	Red flowers on red background #43916258 © bonciutoma - Fotolia.com
	Bedding #25511948 © kim - Fotolia.com
Page 78	Cabin bed #28216208 © Iriana Shiyan - Fotolia.com
Page 79	Luxurious bedroom with view of sea #40409345 © julienguillot - Fotolia.com
Page 83	Interior of a sleeping room 3d image #3709669 © aleksey kashin - Fotolia.com
Page 84	Seamless pattern birds in ethnic graphic style #44342308 © Terriana - Fotolia.com

|191

Page 84	Rot Gelb Orange Check Red seamless scottish pattern #34464251 © Albachiaraa - Fotolia.com
Page 85	United colors of emotion #34519590 © ultrakreativ - Fotolia.com
	Seamless pattern with autumn maple leaves #42577183 © Terriana - Fotolia.com
	Seamless background - Africa #42306704 © benjaminlion - Fotolia.com
Page 86	Set of 5 Different Autumn's Banners #43723495 © Taiga - Fotolia.com
Page 87	Yellow bedroom #1148747 © Pavel Losevsky - Fotolia.com
Page 88	Spectacles on background with book and reading lamp #8739265 © cosma - Fotolia.com
Page 89	Hotel rooms #33581270 © chenke007 - Fotolia.com
Page 90	Dried autumn leaves #18608777 © Jennifer Jane - Fotolia.com
Page 93	Modern room #20977769 © DIDEM HIZAR - Fotolia.com
Page 96	Modern comfortable interior #4028867 © George Mayer - Fotolia.com
Page 97	Interior design scene #37667134 © oliavlasenko - Fotolia.com
Page 98	Abstract business background waves set #39731574 © andegraund548 - Fotolia.com
Page 99	nterior design of modern white living room #36669665 © kosheen - Fotolia.com
	Seamless pattern with peppers on white background, Print #43951888 © Terriana - Fotolia.com
	Modern interior, red sofa indoor #27227904 © kosheen - Fotolia.com
	Anime bedroom #29839877 © nastazia - Fotolia.com
Page 100	Bright pillows isolated on white #43482840 © caimacanul - Fotolia.com
Page 101	Interior of playroom. #35563291 © poligonchik - Fotolia.com
	Seamless rose #40350234 © lenasineva - Fotolia.com
	Seamless pattern with peppers on light green background #43951911 © Terriana - Fotolia.com
	Floral bedding. #22874837 © karam miri - Fotolia.com
Page 102	Seamless blue orange art macro texture background #40707904 © maxximmm - Fotolia.com
Page 103	Orange stairway on the blue wall #43656253 © Dmitry Koksharov - Fotolia.com
Page 104	Seamless pattern #42247111 © Terriana - Fotolia.com
Page 105	Bedroom interior. #26154527 © poligonchik - Fotolia.com
Page 107	Bienenwachskerzen, Hochformat #26884321 © U. Hardberck - Fotolia.com
Page 108	Durst #390934 © foto.fritz - Fotolia.com
	Yoga Woman #25012749 © Babay - Fotolia.com
	Relaxation and body treatment #30029940 © Mee Ting - Fotolia.com
Page 109	Interior of girl's bedroom. #37580921 © poligonchik - Fotolia.com
Page 110	Print of tulips #42010623 © Terriana - Fotolia.com
Page 112	Seamless pattern with plant motifs flowers and berries #42395066 © Terriana - Fotolia.com
Page 113	Teen's bedroom #20195203 © nastazia - Fotolia.com
Page 114 -	Snail stair #8736047 © bravajulia - Fotolia.com
Page 115	Luxe #31904394 © Myrtille MLB - Fotolia.com
Page 116	Nail Polish. #45086040 © Dmitry Fisher - Fotolia.com
	Colorful flower petal closeup #35399843 © maram – Fotolia.com
Page 117	Shades of pink #25767571 © PAO joke - Fotolia.com
Page 120	Buddha Grunge Face #40873826 © KD-Photo - Fotolia.com
Page 121	Beautiful and modern bedroom interior design. #19455054 © Angel Vasilev - Fotolia.com

Page 123	Bedroom interior #35504060 © Kayros Studio - Fotolia.com
Page 124	Rosy pink interior design plan #10094761 © monamakela.com - Fotolia.com
Page 125	Master bedroom in beige #21137995 © Isaxar - Fotolia.com
Page 126	Bedroom #20770763 © Monster - Fotolia.com
Page 127	Bedroom #20769764 © Monster - Fotolia.com
Page 128	Beautiful pink sunset or sunrise #14446224 © Jaren Wicklund - Fotolia.com
Page 130	Interior decoration repair upholstery planning #41168033 © severija kirilovaite - Fotolia.com
Page 130	Cocooning violet #19550757 © SFG - Fotolia.com
Page 131	Modern bedroom. #30590565 © poligonchik - Fotolia.com
Page 134	Lavender wellness collection #33418315 © victoria p. - Fotolia.com
Page 135	Bedroom with flowers #44262743 © liatris - Fotolia.com
Page 136	Bedroom in pastels #44221077 © Magda Fischer - Fotolia.com
Page 138	Bedroom #11058254 © Irina MANSIEUX - Fotolia.com
Page 139	Sandwich #39580137 © Viktorija - Fotolia.com
	Chamomile tea #38728328 © gudrun - Fotolia.com
	Interior of boy's room. #35669784 © poligonchik - Fotolia.com
Page 140	Decorative painting #1461452 © kameel - Fotolia.com
Page 141	Green minimal bed #29841114 © nastazia - Fotolia.com
Page 142	Wellness #24140372 © PhotoSG - Fotolia.com
Page 143	Overwater villa, Maldives #21114651 © forcdan - Fotolia.com
Page 144	Planning decoration in turquoise #6163988 © monamakela.com - Fotolia.com
Page 145	Rest in Paradise #25864038 © Murat Subatli - Fotolia.com
	Modern Bedroom #33851059 © Stocksnapper - Fotolia.com
Page 146	Luxurious bathroom with clawfoot tub #3433516 © Wollwerth Imagery - Fotolia.com
Page 147	Modern living-room #26421711 © poligonchik - Fotolia.com
Page 148	Decorative Composition #20480727 © PAO joke - Fotolia.com
Page 150	Hand crafted jewelry #16223321 © Elenathewise - Fotolia.com
Page 151	Master bedroom #33091755 © kaowenhua - Fotolia.com
Page 152	Colorful cushions on the bed #5038819 © Nicolaas Weber - Fotolia.com
Page 153	Assorted herbs and spices #38759488 © sjhuls - Fotolia.com
Page 156	Lamp #3175835 © Jakob Jeske - Fotolia.com
Page 157	Bedroom #36962779 © fongfong - Fotolia.com
Page 158	Composition of stones and sand #39787454 © pixarno - Fotolia.com
Page 160	Empty beige new bedroom interior. #40571292 © Iriana Shiyan - Fotolia.com
	White interior decoration plan #6164118 © monamakela.com - Fotolia.com
Page 161	Modern bathroom #27624552 © Maksim Kostenko - Fotolia.com
	Pattern of Leaves #41132734 © Fabi K. - Fotolia.com
	Home textiles #38901396 © click - Fotolia.com
	Modern design of a bedroom #41500890 © Sergey Yarochkin - Fotolia.com
Page 162	Drawers #27765396 © Régis Rousseau - Fotolia.com
Page 163	Interior of nursery. #44317813 © poligonchik - Fotolia.com

Page 164   Teddy goes to bed #717132 © Eric Gevaert - Fotolia.com
Page 165   Two hearts in natural colors #34359823 © Jeanette Dietl - Fotolia.com
Page 167   Cat behind curtain © tschecki #44855489 - Fotolia.com
Page 168   Bedroom #20770486 © Monster - Fotolia.com
Page 169   Beautiful young woman standing by the win #29335998 © Sergey Skleznev - Fotolia.com
Page 170   Guestroom #26237369 © SibylleMohn - Fotolia.com
Page 171   Empty room with window #10232725 © Daniel Bujack - Fotolia.com
Page 172   Interior design #42295819 © sergey02 - Fotolia.com
Page 173   Modern bedroom with large window #40254114 © aaphotograph - Fotolia.com
Page 174   blinds #2454074 © Iva Janiga - Fotolia.com
Page 175   Yellow chair in front of a gray wall #31209811 © virtua73 - Fotolia.com
Page 176   Small modern bedroom #38248090 © aaphotograph - Fotolia.com
Page 177   Luxury vintage bathtub © captainlookchoob #37835102
Page 178   Modern design interior of bedroom #31162812 © elizamari - Fotolia.com
Page 179   Luxurious bedroom #6689717 © Dmitry Koksharov - Fotolia.com
Page 180   Interior view of a bedroom with a view of the lake #40409212 © julienguillot - Fotolia.com
Page 181   Good Morning! #12986394 © Peter D. - Fotolia.com
Page 183   Pillows in Hotel bedroom #43427707 © Perseomedusa - Fotolia.com
Page 184   Bed time #41661149 © laurent dambies - Fotolia.com
Page 185   Bed room #45043507 © michaelstockfoto - Fotolia.com
Page 185   Hotel bed #39669899 © Alexey Stiop - Fotolia.com

Disclaimer

Please note that all information in this book, including photographs, patterns, designs, projects and instructions, is only intended for the reader. It is forbidden to use this information for commercial purposes without the written permission of the copyright holders. A list of photographers and interior designers is included in this book, as well as the contact address of the author.

Although every precaution has been taken to make certain that all the information in this book is correct, due to the skills and conditions of the readers, the author cannot take the responsibility for any damages or injuries that may occur from using this book. Despite very careful selection and examination of the websites recommended in this book, please note that the author takes no liability for the content of external links. The owners of the linked websites and pages are responsible for their content.

About the author

Doreen Frances Richmond is a Color Consultant For Interior Design and Architecture I.A.C.C. She lives in Munich, Germany where she trains business owners and professionals alike in the theme of color design and color psychology. Doreen´s blog can be found at: www.colorcherish.com

For information about her seminars and for speaking engagements, please contact Doreen through her blogsite.

IBSN Nr. 978-1480026957

Author:
Doreen Frances Richmond, Munich Germany
doreen.richmond@t-online.de

Printed by:
Create Space, USA
Graphic Design:
Frauke Deutsch, Munich, Germany

Contact Author:
Please visit her Blog www.colorcherish.com

Printed in Great Britain
by Amazon

82973853R00112